Oliver Martin Johnston

The historical syntax of the atonic personal pronouns in

Italian

Oliver Martin Johnston

The historical syntax of the atonic personal pronouns in Italian

ISBN/EAN: 9783337229306

Printed in Europe, USA, Canada, Australia, Japan

Cover: Foto ©Paul-Georg Meister /pixelio.de

More available books at **www.hansebooks.com**

THE HISTORICAL SYNTAX

OF THE

ATONIC PERSONAL PRONOUNS

IN ITALIAN.

DISSERTATION

Presented to the Board of University Studies of the Johns Hopkins University for the Degree of Doctor of Philosophy

BY

OLIVER MARTIN JOHNSTON.

TORONTO:
ROWSELL & HUTCHISON, 74 AND 76 KING STREET EAST.
1898.

TO
MY DEAR PARENTS,
TO WHOSE CONSTANT ENCOURAGEMENT
I AM GREATLY INDEBTED FOR WHAT I MAY
HAVE ACCOMPLISHED IN MY STUDIES,
THIS MONOGRAPH IS AFFECTIONATELY DEDICATED.

TABLE OF CONTENTS.

	PAGE
INTRODUCTION	xi-xii
I.—CHAPTER I.—Mixing of Tonic and Atonic Forms	1-27
A.—Examples of irregular occurrences in the texts examined	1-9
1.—Tonic forms in atonic position	1-7
a.—Single tonic pronouns in proclitic position	1-2
b.—Single tonic forms in enclitic position; attached to the verb	3
c.—Single tonic forms in enclitic position; not attached to the verb	3-4
d.—Double forms in proclitic position, in which the tonic vowel of the second pronoun has been carried to the first pronoun	4-6
e.—Double forms in enclitic position, in which the tonic vowel of the second pronoun has been carried to the first pronoun	6-7
2.—Atonic forms in tonic position	8
3.—Union of two atonic forms in combinations where the second pronoun is usually tonic	8-9
a.—In proclitic position	8-9
b.—In enclitic position	9
B.—Résumé	9-12
1.—Tonic pronouns in atonic position	9-10
a.—Single tonics in proclitic position	9-10
b.—Single tonics in enclitic position	10-11
aa.—Attached to the verb	10
bb.—Not attached to the verb	10-11
2.—Atonic forms in tonic position	11
3.—Double forms, in which the first is generally written as a tonic, but sometimes both are atonic	11-12
a.—In proclitic position	11
b.—In enclitic position	12
C.—Discussion of tonic pronouns in atonic position	12-24
1.—In proclitic position	13-15
a.—*me, te, se*—remnants of the Latin accusative.	13-15
b.—*el* for *il*, a dialectical form	15

TABLE OF CONTENTS.

	PAGE
2.—*me* and *te* in enclitic position	15-17
a.—Attached to the verb	15-16
b.—*me* and *te* following immediately after the verb and not attached	17
3.—Tonic forms that have a similar explanation in proclitic and enclitic position	17-24
a.—*ne*, the first person plural	17-18
b.—*noi, voi, lui, lei, loro*	19-20
c.—*me lo*, etc. ; *te lo*, etc. ; *se lo*, etc. ; *me ne, te ne, se ne ; glielo*, etc. ; *gliene*	20-22
d.—The second pronoun in these combinations (no. c) is tonic	23-24
D.—Discussion of atonic forms in tonic position	24-25
1.—Introduced through dialectical influence	24-25
E.—Extent of the mixing of tonic and atonic forms	25
F.—Time of disappearance	25-26
Conclusions	26-27
II.—Chapter II.—Uses of Atonic Forms in Atonic Position	28-60
A.—Examples of regular occurrences in texts examined	28-39
1.—General constructions	28-31
a.—Single proclitics	28-29
aa.—Before finite verbs	28-29
bb.—Before infinitives	29
b.—Single enclitics	30
aa.—Attached to infinitives	30
bb.—Attached to imperatives	30
c.—Constructions common to proclitic and enclitic position	30-31
2.—Special constructions	31-39
a.—Single proclitics	31-35
b.—Single enclitics with finite verbs	35-36
c.—Enclitics with *che, dietro, addosso, dreto*	36-37
d.—Constructions common to proclitic and enclitic position	37-38
e.—Double atonics, in which the direct precedes the indirect object in combinations where *mi, ti, ci, vi* stand next to *lo*, etc., *la*, etc.	38-39
B.—Résumé	39-43
a.—Single proclitics	39-41
b.—Single enclitics	41-42
c.—Constructions common to proclitic and enclitic position	42
d.—Pronouns of address	42-43
e.—Double atonics, in which the direct precedes the indirect object	43

	PAGE
C.—Discussion of single atonics	43-57
1.—In proclitic position	43-45
a.—Nominatives *i'*, *i*, *no'*, *vo'*, *e'*, *gli*, *la*, *l'*, (= *la*), *le*	43-45
b.—Atonic pronouns in hiatus	45
2.—In enclitic position	45-46
a.—Origin of *mi*, *ti*, *si*	45-46
3.—Constructions common to proclitic and enclitic position (or partly proclitic and partly enclitic)	46-57
a.—Mixing of gender, number, and person	46-48
aa.—Masculine for feminine	46-47
bb.—Singular for plural	47
cc.—*si* (= *ci*)	47-48
b.—Uses of *il*, *'l*, and *lo* before the verb	48-49
c.—Position of atonic pronouns with finite verbs	49-50
d.—Position of atonic pronouns with infinitives	50-51
aa.—Infinitives not dependent upon verbs	50
bb.—Infinitives depending on verbs	51
e.—Reflexives	51-52
f.—Dative constructions	52-54
aa.—Dative with verbs	52-53
bb.—Indirect object after adjectives	53
cc.—Dative of the possessor	53
dd.—Possessive strengthened by the dative	53-54
ee.—Dative of the agent	54
g.—Atonic pronouns of address	54-57
D.—Discussion of double atonics	57-58
1.—Arrangement	57-58
Conclusions	58-60
Bibliography	61-66

SYNTACTICAL HISTORY

OF THE

ATONIC PERSONAL PRONOUNS

IN ITALIAN

FROM THE MIDDLE OF THE THIRTEENTH
TO THE END OF
THE NINETEENTH CENTURY.

INTRODUCTION.

The atonic forms existing in the texts examined are:—

SINGULAR.

	SUBJECT.	DIRECT OBJECT.	INDIRECT OBJECT.
1st Person	i', i.	mi, m'.	mi, m'.
2nd Person		ti, t'.	ti, t'.
3rd Per. m.	e', gli.	il, 'l, lo, l'.	gli, gl', li, i.
3rd Per. fem.	la, l'.	la, l'.	le, gli.
Reflexives		si, s'.	si, s'.

PLURAL.

	SUBJECT.	DIRECT OBJECT.	INDIRECT OBJECT.
1st Person	no'.	ci, c'.	ci, c'.
2nd Person	vo'.	vi, v'.	vi, v'.
3rd Per. m.	e', gli.	gli[1], li, i.	
3rd Per. fem.	le.	le.	le.
Reflexives		si, s'.	si, s'.

The table given above represents the general usage in the texts consulted; however, in a historical examination of proclitics and enclitics in Italian (in addition to the regular atonic constructions), numerous examples are found of the corresponding tonic pronouns that occur in unaccented position and which are governed as direct and indirect objects of verbs, just as in the case of atonics. Similar researches will also show that atonic *mi* and *ti* were occasionally adopted in tonic position.

This variance in usage makes it necessary, first of all, that a full collection of the irregularities mentioned be

---

[1] The tonic form *loro* early supplanted the plurals *gli, li, le*, and is now employed regularly in conjunctive position.

made, and explanations be offered for the confusion and final separation of tonic and atonic forms, preparatory to a treatment of the special constructions of the unaccented pronouns, which constructions will then unfold themselves naturally in the light of Historical Grammar.

Following the atonic forms, already indicated (*cf.* p. xi), through the texts examined for the present study, it will be noted that the pronouns given were not all employed to the same extent by the authors of the various periods, and many rules will be noted of grammatical structure widely different from those existing in Modern Italian. The application of this historical method to the syntactical point in question not only brings to knowledge constructions not hitherto mentioned by Italian grammarians, but classifies all the material found, determines the relative frequency of irregular and special uses by actual count, and, at the same time, not only renders possible rational explanations of the diverse syntactical phenomena, through a comparison of the individual authors of the different epochs of the Italian itself, but, going behind the oldest Italian monuments, enables one to seek the origin of any given Italian construction in the Latin, wherever it is possible to identify the Italian representative with the Latin original.

Thus, the Syntactical History of the atonic personal pronouns may be divided into two parts.

In the first chapter the mixing of the accented and unaccented forms will be noted, and suggestions and explanations for such confusions will be attempted. In the second chapter will be traced the regular uses of proclitics and enclitics, with special reference to the origin and growth of constructions as influenced by individual authors.

I now wish to acknowledge my indebtedness to Professor F. J. A. Davidson, of Leland Stanford Jr. University, for kindly reading the proofs of my dissertation.

CHAPTER I.

Mixing of Tonic and Atonic Forms.

THE atonic personal pronouns are the only ones employed as direct and indirect object of a verb and always stand next to the verb upon which they throw their accent, either leaning forward as proclitics or casting their accent back as enclitics[1]. Hence, the occurrence of any pronouns in conjunctive position, except the list of atonics already given (*cf.* p. xi.), will be treated as an abnormal use of tonic for atonic forms; in like manner the use of atonic forms after prepositions, or apart from the verb, will be considered as an equal encroachment of atonic upon the domain of tonic pronouns. With the position of the accented and unaccented Italian pronouns thus defined, irregularities arising from a crossing of the two will be easily recognized, tested and eliminated.

My plan is to mention each construction separately. After a full list of examples has been given, a résumé will follow, indicating the number of times a given phenomenon is found in each author examined.

A.—Examples of irregular occurrences in texts examined.

   1.—Tonic forms in atonic position.
     a.—Single tonic pronouns in proclitic position.

el = *il* : B[2], p. 145.
    C'ormai le donne ch'*el* vedranno morto
    Ciascuna più pietanza avranno in core.

me = *mi* : O, Purg. XXI, 18,
    Poi cominciò: nel beato concilio
    Ti ponga in pace la verace corte,
    Che *me* rilega nell 'eterno esilio ;
      DD, p. 3,
    E poi *me* disse : guarda el Lupatello.

---

[1] For the occasional occurrence of the shortened nominatives *i'*, *i*, *no'*, *vo'*, *e'*, *gli*, *la*, *l'*, *le* as proclitics in the texts examined compare p. 45.

[2] For the use of the letters *A*, *B*, *C*, etc., in giving reference to the authors, compare p. 61.

noi = *ci* : U, 8, 3,
 noi ha lasciati ;
  G, p. 28,
 tredici staia e mezo di o grano o di farina,
 qual *noi* piacese.

ne = *ci* : QQ, Atto 3, Sc. 4,
 Perchè, crudo destino,
 Ne disunisci tu, s'Amor *ne* stringe ;
  U, 1, 1,
 il mandarlo fuori di casa
 così infermo *ne* sarebbe gran biasmo.

te = *ti* : U, 8, 7,
 te ha fatto agghiacciare ;
  W¹, kiiii6,
 io *te* parlo.

vai = *vi* : P, I, 231,
 Così me, Donna, il *voi* veder, felice
 Fa in questo breve, e frale viver mio ;
  U, 6, 10,
 Se *voi* piace.

se = *si* : L, p. 205.
 el tesoro diroma si era consumato en la guerra
  danibal ke non *se* trova da potere pagare li
  cavalieri.

lui = *lo* : O, *Inf.* XXVI, 78,
 In questa forma *lui* parlare audivi.

lei = *la* : P, I, 118,
 E *lei* vid'io ferita in mezzo 'l core ;
  U, 2, 8,
 lei hebbero molto cara.

*loro*² = *gli, li, le* : U, 2, 6,
 il suo fiero proponimento *loro* aperse ;
  LL, I, 42,
 E come mi fu tolta, *lor* narrai.

---

[1] In looking for this reference it will be necessary to count six pages forward from folio kiiii, as this system is observed in all editions divided according to folios.

[2] *Cf.* fcotnote, p. xi.

b.—Single tonic forms in enclitic position; attached to the verb,

me in rhyme: P, I, 172,
  E l'angelico canto, e le parole
  Col dolce spirto, ond'io non posso aitar*me*,
  Son l'aura, innanzi a cui mia vita fugge;
    P, I, 236,
  L'aura serena, che fra verdi fronde
  Mormorando a ferir nel volto vie*mme*,
  Fammi risavvenir quand 'Amor diè*mme*
  Le prime piaghe sì dolci e profonde.

me not in rhyme: P, II, 86,
  E però mi son mosso a pregar morte,
  Che mi tolla di qui per far*me* lieto.

ne[1] = *ci*: O, *Inf*. XIII, 87-89,
  Spirito incarcerato, ancor ti piaccia
  Di dir*ne* come l'anima si lega
  In questi nocchi; din*ne*, se tu puoi,
  Se alcuna mai da tai membra si spiega.

te not in rhyme: DD, p. 181,
  Non consentir a far un tal micidio,
  Che sai ch'io t'amo assai piu che tu stessa,
  Per gloriar*te* fatto un altro Ovidio.

c.—Single tonic forms in enclitic position; not attached to the verb.

me = *mi*: U, 5, 4,
  volesse Iddio, che tu non facessi piu morir *me*;
    O, *Inf*. XXIII, 91,
  Poi disser *me*, ecc.

noi = *ci*: O, *Inf*. V, 106,
  Amor condusse *noi* ad una morte.

te = *ti*: I, p. 59,
  L'altrui giustizia non liberà *te*.

voi = *vi*: A, p. 95 V,
  Anchora d'amar *voi* non fui sì acceso.

lui = *lo*: O, *Inf*. XIV, 71,
  Ma, come io dissi *lui*, li suoi dispetti
  Sono al suo petto assai debiti fregi.

---

[1] *Cf*. O, *Inf*. V, 29; *Purg*. V, 30.

lei = la : O, *Inf.* XXI, 19,
   Io vedea lei, ma non vedea in essa
   Ma che le bolle che il bollor levava ;
               U, 2, 8,
   egli imaginava *lei* di bassa condition.

loro = gli, li, le : II, I, 144,
   Mè so quanto il restar fusse *lor* caro ;
               BBB, p. 72, .
non parendo *loro* cosa conveniente che,
a quell'ora, si trattenesse più a lungo.

d.—Double forms in proclitic position in which the tonic vowel of the second pronoun has been carried to the first pronoun.

me lo = m'elo : V. I, 30,
   me lo mostra ;
               II, II, 168,
   Rinaldo *me lo* viene a disturbare.

me la = m'ela : P, II, 119,
   Ben *me la* diè, ma tosto la ritalse ;
               V. I, 29,
   Che *me la* manda chiedendo.

me ne = m'ene : V. I, 22,
   Cristo *me ne* guardi.

ce lo = c'elo : Z, nov. 59,
   Che *ce lo* dia.

ce la = c'ela : NN, p. 189,
   tale è la nostra vita, quale la natura *ce la* dece
      essere poscia che noi venuti ci siamo ;
               NN, p. 101,
   se non che quelle cose, che la fortuna ci dà, esso
      dolci e soavi *ce le* fa essere.

ce ne = c'ene : J, p. 19,
   credemo bene ch'elli *ce ne* farà a piacere ;
               J, p. 21,
   giammái ne *ce ne* miraremo drieto.

te lo = t'elo : V, I, 9,
   io *te lo* dirò ;
               II, II, 32,
   Sai ch'altra volta *te lo* volsi dire.

te la = *t'ela* : V, I, 12,
    io *te la* insegnerò ;
        II, I, 26,
    Io *te la* gratterò, s'il ti bisogna.

te ne = *t'ene* : V, I, 32,
    io *te ne* voglio dire ;
        II, I, 30,
    e'n tulto *te ne* voglio confortare.

ve lo = *v'elo* : V, I, 15,
    io *ve lo* dirò ;
        II, I, 116,
    ve lo conterò.

ve la = *v'ela* : UU, I, 26,
    ve l' ha rubata.

ve ne = *v'ene* : J, p. 60,
    noi non *ve ne* scrivaremo mai piue ;
        V, I, 15,
    Pur che *ve ne* piaccia.

se lo = *s'elo* : K, p. 203,
    ma elli *se lo* sentia si presso,
    che non se ne osava partire ;
        Y, p. 135,
    se li gittò a' piedi.

se la = *s'ela* : H, p. 130,
    di che ognuno *se la* levò ;
        Y, nov. 9,
    se la pregava.

se ne = *s'ene* : BBB, p. 18,
    *se n'*andò.

glielo : V, I, 245,
    glielo chiese ;
        BBB, p. 41,
    glielo raccomandava.

gliela : V, I, 180,
    tu *gliela* donerai ;
        V, I, 92,
    glie la leva.

gliene: V, I, 88,
>Giannetto *glie ne* volle dare venti mila;
>BBB, p. 32,
>certo nessun uomo di giudizio
>*gliene* avrette dato il parere.

e.—Double forms in enclitic position in which the tonic vowel of the second pronoun has been carried to the first pronoun, but both forms being attached to the verb the accent is last.

[1]*me lo = m'elo:* V, I, 30,
>convien*melo* vedere;
>BBB, p. 33,
>raccontate*melo* un poco.

me la = m'ela: LL, V, 139,
>levar*mela*;
>BBB, p. 73,
>date*mele* ora.

me ne = m'ene: V, I, 55,
>menò*mene*;
>BBB, p. 154,
>impicciar*mene*.

ce la = c'ela: DDD, p. 112,
>discorriamo*cela* fra noi.

ce ne = c'ene: NN, p. 252,
>pura contentezza nel sonno medesimo
>procacciamo, e a pascere incomincian*cene*
>così sognando.

te lo = t'elo: V, I, 58,
>questo è un dire, tien*telo* sempre mai;
>II, IV, 223,
>A dir*telo* ad un tratto, io nol vo' fare.

te la = t'ela: BBB, p. 209,
>dir*tela*.

te ne = t'ene: KK, II, 230,
>tornar*tene*;
>KK, II, 263,
>piglia*tene*.

---

[1] *me lo, me la*, etc., are unaccented when joined to the verb, but are treated under the head of tonics, because their form is the same as the corresponding combinations before the verb where the second pronoun is tonic.

ve lo = v'elo: K, p. 104,
   diròvvelo assai brevemente;
       BBB, p. 308,
   dovevo dirvelo.
ve la = v'ela: BBB, p. 110,
   lasciandovela.
ve ne = v'ene: BBB, p. 72,
   ma anche voi avevate promesso
   di non fare scandoli di
   remettervene al padre;
       BBB, p. 60,
   non ho più bisogno di riguardi a
   parlarvene.
se lo = s'elo: Y, nov. 166,
   trovandoselo;
       BBB, p. 67,
   presentandosegli davanti i due sposi.
se la = s'ela: DDD, p. 14,
   dunque, a che serve pigliarsela a cuore?
       BBB, p. 384,
   cominciò a prendersela con Perpetua.
se ne = s'ene: BBB, p. 58,
   andarsene;
       BBB, p. 58,
   liberarsene.
glielo: V, I, 58,
   donoglielo;
       BBB, p. 240,
   il fazzoletto veniva
   a soffogarglielo in gola.
gliela: V, I, 177,
   fregogliela;
       BBB, p. 239,
   quand'anche non l'avesse mai veduta,
   a insegnargliela, non la poteva sbagliare.
gliene: V, I, 207,
   egli promettendogliene;
       BBB, p. 94,
   e quasi per chiedergliene scusa.

2.—Atonic forms in tonic position.

mi^1 = *me*: U, 6, 4,
voi non l'havrì da *mi*, Donna
Brunetta, voi non l'havrì da *mi*;
Z, nov. 74,
messer Bernabo disse: Messer l'ambasciadore, sali
su quel cavallo, e verra' con *mi* parlando.

ti^2 = *te*: YY, I, 37,
Onde fora tutti dò de sta cosa.
mi per elezion, *ti* per obbedienza;
YY, I, p. 37,
ti per imperar a viver con cautela, con più giudizio,
con più rispetto a te pare.

3.—Union of two atonic forms in combinations where the second pronoun usually shows a tonic vowel.

a.—In proclitic position.

tilo: F, p. 30,
senacha disse: quello che tuo sai
insegnalo a chi *ti l'*adimanda.

tine: F, p. 21,
Salomone disse: tucte le cose fae
con consilio, e no *ti ne* penterai;
F, p. 90,
ti ne dirò.

sigli: BB, p. 20,
La donzella Carduino a chiamato,
E in tal modo *sigli* prese a dire.

glilo: V, I, 41,
gli lo disse;
LL, I, 207,
E gli diede intenzion ch '1 di seguente
Gli lo trarrebbe fuor di quello stato.

glila: LL, I, 3,
Il savio imperator ch'estinguer volse
Un grave incendio, fu che *gli la* tolse;
LL, I, 205,
In odio *gli la* pose.

---

[1] *Cf.* YY, I, pp. 36, 38, 67; Z, nov. 65 and nov. 69.
[2] *Cf.* YY, p. 41.

gline : LL, I, 260,
   Se trova alcun che vegghi, sospirando
   Gli ne dipinge l'abito e la forma.

b.—In enclitic position.

milo : GG, p. 312,
   dissi*mil* ecc.;
   V, I, 35,
   io m'ucciderò io stessa per levar*migli* dinanzi.

sigli : V, I, 131,
   e per ciò ricorevano a lui per
   l'aiuto suo, raccomando *sigli* per
   amor di Dio.

glilo : Z, nov. 124,
   cercò di quello, dov'era
   il busecchio, e mando*glilo ;*
   Z, nov. 166,
   mostrando di voler*glilo*
   ficcare nel viso.

lila : Y, p. 34,
   far*lila.*

line : M, nov. 26,
   et offerse*line* duo marchi.

B.—RÉSUMÉ.

The following table is a résumé of the irregular occurrences noted above. The capital letters represent the authors and the numerals indicate the number of times a given form is found in the author mentioned :—

1.—Tonic pronouns in atonic position.
a.—Single tonics in proclitic position.

   me = mi : A3[1], B9, E, F, L, M, N4, O8, P13, R2, U21, V, W60, Z2, AA2, CC9, DD18, GG3, II2, KK5, LL6, NN5, OO, QQ2, WW3, XX38, ZZ, AAA13.

   noi = ci : B, G, H, K, L, N, U2, CC, II, LL, NN, YY.

---

[1] The numeral placed to the right of a capital letter represents the number of times a form occurs in the author given. If no numeral is expressed the form occurs only once in the author indicated.

ne = ci : M5, O71, P14, U12, W6, DD, EE3,
I17, LL7, MM, NN, PP, QQ5, SS2, TT,
WW3, AAA, FFF2.

te = ti : M, O, P, U, W59, BB, CC3, DD13, GG,
II4, NN, OO2, QQ3, UU, WW3, YY11.
— AAA6, FFF3.

voi = vi : B7, C2, E5, O, P2, U2, CC5, KK4, NN,
SS2, YY.

se = si : B, L9, W4, CC, DD, GG.

lui = lo : B3, F, L4, O12, P2, R2, U26, W2, Y2,
Z, AA, EE, GG, II2, KK3, LL7, NN,
OO4, QQ, SS.

lei = la : B2, C, E2, N, O, P10, S, U29, W, EE3,
GG3, II, LL12, OO, WW2, AAA2, CCC.

el = il : B2, K13, L2, W112, AA, CC, YY3.

loro = gli : E, H, K10, L4, O4, P2, Q, R3, S, U49,
Y2, GG, II21, JJ, LL85, NN5, OO4,
SS, TT, UU4, WW, ZZ2, AAA, BBB,
CCC2.

b.—Single tonics in enclitic position.
aa.—Attached to the verb.

me in rhyme : P23, W5, LL13, TT, YY, CCC.
me not in rhyme : B, L2, P, S2, W8, CC3, KK, NN3, YY8.
ne not in rhyme : O7, II, QQ2.
te not in rhyme : DD.

bb.—Not attached to the verb.

me = mi : B6, E3, F, I, M2, N, O20, P17, R, S,
U7, V5, W15, X, Z8, AA, CC2, FF3,
GG2, II5, KK7, LL4, NN, OO, QQ2,
XX, YY, AAA3, BBB3, DDD2, EEE.

noi = ci : A, C, H, N, O7, R, U5, Z, CC, KK,
NN, SS, YY, AAA, DDD.

te = ti : F4, I, M, O8, P2, U12, V2, W3, X, Z4,
CC, DD, EE, GG5, KK, LL, MM, QQ3,
TT, AAA, BBB2, DDD2.

voi = vi : A3, B6, C, E8, F, N, P7, U3, V, Y, CC,
GG2, LL, NN, OO2, SS, YY2, BBB,
FFF.

lui = *lo* : B2, C, F3, L10, M, N2, O46, P5, S2, U42, V6, W6, X, Y3, Z8, AA, BB2, CC, DD3, FF2, II13, KK7, LL21, MM3, NN, OO3, SS, TT2, UU, BBB5, DDD2.

lei = *la* : B3, C6, E5, K, O13, P22, U25, V2, W2, AA, EE3, GG4, HH, II0, LL26, NN, QQ3, TT4, XX, ZZ, BBB, CCC2.

loro = *li, le, gli* : H32, K, L4, O2, P12, Q9, R6, S47, U50, Y16, GG10, II80, LL92, NN38, OO, SS4, TT9, UU14, ZZ13, AAA, BBB33, CCC3, rule[1] in A, B, C, D, E, F, G, I, J, M, N, T, V, W, X, Z, AA, BB, CC, DD, EE, FF, HH, JJ, KK, MM, PP, QQ, RR, VV, WW, XX, YY, DDD, EEE, FFF.

2.—Atonic forms in tonic position.

mi = *me* : U3, Z7, YY38, FFF.

ti = *te* : YY6.

3.—Double forms where the first is generally written as a tonic, but sometimes both are atonic.

The combinations in which both pronouns are unaccented will be placed to the right of those in which the first form shows a tonic vowel. In all the texts not mentioned in the résumé below, *me lo, te lo, se lo, me ne, te ne, se ne, glielo, gliela, gliene*, etc., are found to the exclusion of *mi lo, ti lo, si lo*, etc[2].

a.—In proclitic position.

	ti lo : F rule.
	ti ne : F rule.
sel : BB3.	*sigli* : BB2.
glielo : Z8, LL8, V11.	*gli lo* : Z4, LL30, V.
	gli la : V, Z3, JJ rule, LL6.
	li le : M rule.
gliene : Z11, FF, LL, UU2.	*gline* : Z2, FF2, JJ rule, LL9, UU2.

---

[1] "Rule" indicates that the construction given is found without variants.

[2] This statement includes all combinations of *mi, ti, si*, with *lo*, etc.; *la*, etc., and *ne* (*cf. melo, mela, te lo, te la, selo, se la, glielo, gliela, gliene*).

b.—In enclitic position.

melo : GG, V3, KK15, PP2.
mil : GG.
mili : J rule.
migli : V, KK, PP.
sigli : V rule.
gli lo : Z rule.
li la : Y rule.
line : M rule.

C.—*Discussion of tonic pronouns in atonic position.*

A construction common to all the periods of Italian literature is the use of tonic for atonic forms whenever it is desired to render emphatic the person or thing upon which falls the action of the verb[1].

Eliminating this general construction, the numerous occurrences of tonics for atonics indicated in the list of examples and résumé given on the preceding pages, now require special explanation.

Considered as a whole, three possible reasons for these irregularities suggest themselves :—

First, it is to be noted that this confusion of forms existed in a greater proportion in the early texts than in those of a later date[2]. In the formative period of the language, before the laws of syntax became definitely fixed under the influence of great epoch-making poets and novelists, a finished grammar, the product of centuries of natural growth and linguistic criticism, is not to be expected. In this transitional period of the Italian speech, as is shown by the endless discussion of grammarians upon the smallest as well as the most important questions of grammar, there was a lack of definite rules governing the syntactical structure, and a want of clear differentiation between the different sets of pronouns, often leaving writers in doubt as to which was right and which was wrong. This uncertainty as to the real distinction between the

---

[1] NN, p. 127 : Ma se io amo *lei*, e se ella
Me ama, non è tuttavia ;
AAA, I, 142 : uccidi, uccidi *me*.

[2] *Cf.* résumé, pp. 9-12.

function of tonic and atonic forms may have led to the frequent substitution of the former for the latter.

Secondly, it is to be remarked that in almost all the texts where this mixing occurs the pronouns under discussion frequently stand next to a verb governed either by an expressed or omitted preposition. By the side of such expressions as *a me*[1], *a te*[2], *a se*, *a noi*[3], *a voi*[4], *a lui*[5], *a lei piace* are found *me*[6], *te*[7], *se*, *noi*[8], *voi*[9], *lui*[10], *lei piace*. Thus, by analogy these tonic pronouns, standing already in conjunctive position and employed as the indirect object of a preposition, may have induced the writer to adopt the same forms as direct and indirect object of a verb, thereby simplifying morphology by the use of a single form in both accented and unaccented position, and, at the same time, carrying out the general tendency toward leveling and generalizing in Italian forms.

In the third place, tonic *me, te, se* may have been used as conjunctives through the influence of dialects like the Venetian, which shows regularly an *e* instead of an *i* in the pretonic and postonic syllable. In the comedies of Goldoni[11], representing the popular speech of Italy, are introduced Venetian characters, who invariably interchange tonic and atonic pronouns.

Any one of the suggestions offered might explain theoretically the irregular occurrences in question, but the following explanations seem more tenable in the light of the historic growth of the Italian language.

1.—In proclitic position.

a.—me, te, se—remnants of the Latin accusative.

If we should admit according to D'Ovidio[12] that *mi, ti, si* arose from a mixing of the Latin dative and accusative,

---

[1] Q, p. 16 : se a *me* convenesse andare ecc.
[2] I, p. 8 : *a te* darai di persona.
[3] Q, p. 3 : a *noi* parano utili.
[4] NN, p. 55 : a *voi* piace.
[5] P, I, 155 : a *lui* piace.
[6] O, Purg. XVI, 143 : *me* convien partirmi.
[7] N, p. 12 : Ove *te* piace.
[8] G, p. 28 : tredici staia e mezo di o grano
O di farina, qual *noi* piacese.
[9] J, p. 3 : Se *voi* piace.
[10] L, p. 217 : ca *lui* piacesse.
[11] YY, I, p. 10, *ve* servirò.
[12] *Archivio Glottologico Italiano*, vol. IX, p. 67.

resulting finally in the generalizing of the Latin dative case, beginning, for example, with such forms as *mi*, in *mi pare*, where the *mi* is the regular dative and afterward carried by analogy to *mi* in the accusative ; as, in *mi vide*, we would not for a moment suppose that this analogy was complete from the beginning ; but would naturally expect to find *me*, etc., by the side of *mi*, etc., at least, in the earliest texts. The argument from analogy, as given above, might explain the pronouns, *mi*, *ti*, *si*, and the analogy would, if accepted, account for the occurrence of the double forms *mi*, etc., and *me*, etc., in atonic position, but it is unnecessary to resort to an explanation based on analogy when a phonetic one is possible.

A better solution of the question is that based on the statement of Meyer-Lübke[1], who says : "Die tonlosen Objektspronomina lauten für den Singular der zwei ersten Personen *mi, ti, si* streng nach den Lautregeln, wonach tonloses *e* zu *i* wird para. 123." Taking this statement as a point of departure, it is evident that a leveling period was gone through before the final adoption of the single *i*-form ; for the passage of pretonic $e > i$ was not complete in the earliest Tuscan monuments. Hence, we would be greatly surprised if we should not find an occasional substitution of *e* for *i* until the law of pretonics became definitely fixed and understood in the language. An argument supporting this supposition is the frequent occurrence in Old Italian of *e* for *i* in the pretonic syllable not only in the pronouns, but also in other parts of speech[2].

Now, if, according to Meyer-Lübke[3], the pronouns *mi, ti, si* derive directly from Latin *me, te, se*, any form showing the original *e* in pretonic position will be explained as a remnant of the Latin accusative. The persistence of this case in Italian is not strange ; Italy being the home of Latin, and Italian writers using it instead of their own language to a very late date, it is natural that Latin forms

---

[1] It. Gram., ¶ 370.

[2] *Cf. Crestomazia Italiana dei Primi Secoli.*
Per Ernesto Monaci. Fascicolo Primo.
Città di Castello, 1889, p. 169, line 23 (A), ritenere ; line 23 (B), retenere ; p. 184, line 53, desmonta ; p. 182, line 87, segnoria.
Cf. also L, p. 199 : retornare ; p. 204, remanere.
R, p. 203 : *el* più sicuro ; p. 198, *el* suo tener.

[3] It. *Gram.*, ¶ 370.

should live on in Italian. Just as the Latin neuter plurals[1] *mia, tua, sua,* were preserved by the side of *miei,* etc.; *mie,* etc., so were the accusative forms *me, te, se* kept for a time by the side of the new atonic formations *mi, ti, si.*

 b.—el for *il* a dialectical form.

 The use of *el* for *il* (< Lat. ILLUM) as direct object of a verb is non-Tuscan, for the reason that in this dialect Latin *i* always remains in the pretonic[2] syllable. Then, since this form is found chiefly in texts where popular and dialectical occurrences are common (*cf.* K, L[3], W[4], AA, CC, YY), it is reasonable to suppose that it is a simple borrowing from some dialect in which it is a natural growth. Now, because the dialects of Southern France[5] show this form and because in W (an Italian text in which this phenomenon occurs one hundred and twelve times) is introduced a character who speaks in Provençal, it is very probable that this was the dialect to make the loan.

 2.—*me* and *te* in enclitic position.
 a.—Attached to the verb.

PREVIOUS TREATMENT.

 Francesco Fortunio[6], while defining the various rules for the use of pronouns, says: " la quarta regola serà che questi pronomi oblichi *me, te, se* convertono *e* in *i* quando si congiongon al verbo immediatamente, come, dissemi, fecemi, consumati. Overo quando *l* o vero *r* precede *i* che ad et altro modo si dice, come ferirmi e ferirme, farmi, farme, valmi, valme." My objection to this statement is that it is simply an attempt to make a rule out of a mere coincidence. Perhaps this explanation occurred to the grammarian, because, in many cases, where the pronoun is united with a verb, it is joined to an infinitive, where the

---

 [1] *Cf.* L. Emil Menger, "The Historical Development of the Possessive Pronouns in Italian," pp. 28, 29.
 [2] Meyer-Lübke, *It. Gr.,* ¶ 123.
 [3] p. 198 : essa la terra *ei* diede.
 [4] U r : Poi *si* traemo per la drita via.
 [5] *Cf.* Bartsch, *Chrestomathie Provençale.* Elberfeld, 1868, p. 419.
 [6] *Regole Grammaticali della Volgar Lingua,* Siena, 1533, p. 17.

r naturally precedes. However, the occurrences in the texts consulted show that the letter preceding the pronoun attached, was of no importance[1].

While discussing this same question, Jacopo Gabriello[2] remarks: "il te veramente non è stato da alcuno scrittore usato finiente ne la *e*, dico al verbo vicino, o ne le rime, o altrove che egli cada, perchè da lui lontano sempre in *e* termina. Il che certo mi pare cosa nuova a dover dire, che se io dico desiderar*me*, perchè non mi si dee conceder medesimente il dire, desiderar*te*?" This grammarian attempts no explanation of the point in question, but simply states that *me*, and not *te*, can occur in enclitic position.

Upon the development of *me* in postonic position D'Ovidio[3] says: "gli aitar*me*, par*me* ecc. poet. (unico es. nella D. C. e il *d'altro non calme* del Purg. VIII 12), non so se possan tenersi strascichi d'una fase anteriore, o non piuttosto si riducano a semplici applicazioni della forma tonica (*cfr. dissi lui, lor dissi*), agevolate dall' esempio del *me* ecc. di altri dialetti (roman., pugliese ecc.) ed anche dalle frequenti alternative d' -*i* ed- e ne'nomi e verbi (*tu gride = gridi* ecc.)." The theories of the scholar just quoted are suggestive and may have a practical value in the solution of the point in hand; however, for the reason that the material collected supports neither of the conjectures offered, one is justified in seeking another explanation for the union of tonic *me* and *te* with verbs.

These forms were first attached to the verb for rhyme.

Of the sixty-two occurrences of *me* and *te* joined to the verb in the texts consulted, forty-four[4] are in rhyme, fourteen others in poetry and the remaining four in prose works (L and S), where the substitution of *e*[5] for atonic *i* is frequent. This makes it evident that these forms first arose in this position for the sake of rhyme, and were afterward carried by analogy, aided by poetic license, to constructions not in rhyme.

---

[1] *Cf.* W, aiiv : Et aparve*me* chosse nel dormire ;
    aiiii5, missi*me* alhor per la monstrata via.
[2] *Regole Grammaticali*, venetia, 1548, fol. Dij.
[3] *Archiv. Glott. It.*, p. 70, n. 3.
[4] *Cf.* P, I, 172 :
    Col dolce spirto, ond'io non posso aitar*me*,
    Son l'aura, innanzi a cui mia vita fugge.
[5] *Cf.* L, p. 204 : *el* fratello ; *cf. el* for il in S, edition of Bologna, 1490.

b.—*me* and *te* following immediately after the verb and not attached.

A suggestion that might explain the occurrence of all tonic pronouns in this position is that they may have been employed here for the purpose of individualizing in a more marked way the person or object receiving the action of the verb for clearness and distinction.

However, since the atonic forms generally emphasize the persons sufficiently well, it is very probable that the use of *me* and *te* in such constructions represents a mere development of tonic forms in atonic position[1].

3.—Tonic forms that have a similar explanation in proclitic and enclitic position.

a.—*ne*, the first person plural.

Caix[2], while discussing the origin of the first and second person plural, gives the following developments : *noi*, *voi* > *no'*, *vo'* > *no*, *vo* > *ne*, *ve* (by analogy to *me*, *te*, *se*) > *ci*, *vi* (in Tuscan by anal. to *mi*, *ti*, *si*); then, on account of a confusion with *ne* (< indĕ) *ni* remained as *ne* until finally supplanted by *ci*.

Opposing this theory is the statement of D'Ovidio[3], who says : " Toccando poi anche delle forme atoniche del plurale, noi persisteremo risolutamente a credere, che l' it. ne per'noi, a noi', o vi per 'voi, a voi' sieno semplicemente gli avverbi (inde, ibi)."

A similar opinion is that of Meyer-Lübke[4], who claims that the pronominal forms *ci* and *vi* have the same origin as adverbial *ci* and *vi*, and identifies *ne* (=*noi*, *a noi*) with *ne* (< INDĔ).

The explanation proposed by the last two authorities quoted is doubtless the correct one, being supported by the actual existence of INDE[5] in Italian texts, meaning " us," " to us." But, granting the truth of the hypothesis, that

---

[1] *Cf.* O, *Inf.* XXIII, 91 : Poi disser *me* ecc. ;
Par. XXIV, 152, Così, benedicendomi cantando ;
Tre volte cinse *me*, si com'io tacque.
Inf. XXIII, 50, Come il Maestro mio per quel vivagno,
Portandosene *me* sopra il suo petto.

[2] *Origini della Lingua Poetica Italiana.* Firenze, 1880, ¶¶ 93 and 207.

[3] *Archiv. Glott. It.*, vol. IV., p. 77.

[4] *Cf. It. Gram.*, ¶ 370.

[5] Compare Meyer-Lübke, *It. Gram.*, ¶ 370.

ne, the first person plural, does derive directly from Latin INDE, the question still remains unsettled as to why the form *ne*, being employed regularly as the pretonic and postonic syllable, shows an *e* instead of an *i*.

Neither of the theories offered accounts for the persistence of this *e* of *ne* in atonic position.

Now, the only construction in which *ne* is phonetic is when it is used in enclitic position, where postonic[1] ĕ (*cf.* INDE) remains as distinguished from pretonic[2] ĕ, which regularly > *i*. However, because the occurrences of *ne* (= *noi, a noi*) noted in the texts are mainly proclitic[3], it would not be a logical deduction to say that the examples in pretonic position were fashioned upon the comparatively few enclitic uses. In like manner, one may safely hazard the statement that *ne*, the first person plural, could not have taken its *e* from adverbial *ne* (< INDE), since this adverbial *ne* is used also in unaccented position along by the side of the regular atonic forms *ci* and *vi* and should itself > *ni*. Nor can pronominal and adverbial *ne* be analogical buildings upon the conjunction *ne*, if we accept the theory of Meyer-Lübke[4], where he says: " L'opposé de *et*, c'est-à-dire *nec*, fait encor plus de difficulté: l'italien *ne* semble être une forme atone."

A better suggestion to account for this irregular development is to suppose that *ne* for *ni* arose first in constructions like *me ne parlò* (= m'enne parlò)[5], where the second form is regularly tonic[6] and that the *ne* in *m'enne, t'enne, s'enne*, etc , was afterward carried to constructions where the single form *ne* was employed as pronoun or adverb; as, *ne parlò*.

The conjunction *ne* is then a further analogical growth upon the *ne* and *m'enne*, etc., above indicated.

---

[1] *Cf.* Meyer-Lübke, *It. Gr.*, ¶ 106.
[2] *Cf.* Meyer-Lübke, *It. Gr.*, ¶ 123.
[3] *Cf.* Table, pp. 9-12.
[4] *Grammaire des Longues Romanes*, Paris, 1890. Vol. I., ¶ 613.
[5] *Cf.* m'elo, t'elo, m'ene, t'ene, ecc., p. 21.
[6] *Cf.* p. 23.

b.—*noi, voi, lui, lei, loro*[1].

The frequent use of these tonic pronouns for the corresponding unaccented ones is a simple application[2] of tonic forms in atonic position. Just as *ello*[3] and *ella*[4] were used in Old Italian for the articles *lo* and *la*, so were tonic *noi, voi, lui, lei, loro* often substituted for atonic *ci, vi, lo, la, gli*, etc.

POSITION OF *loro*.

With the exception of *loro* the pronouns mentioned above have always been placed either before or after their governing verb.

Until the present century the place occupied by *loro* in the sentence seems to have been an uncertain and doubtful one. The Italian grammarians[5], in general, have given the rule that it should follow rather than precede its verb.

By comparing the table (pp. 9-12), it will be seen that the construction with *loro* both before the verb and *loro* after the verb were admissible until about the eighteenth century. It will be further noted that some writers, even in Old Italian, used the latter construction to the exclusion of the former, and in the nineteenth century it seems to be a generally accepted law that *loro* shall follow its verb.

The occurrences of *loro* before the verb may be explained either as Latin survivals, or as being fashioned upon possessive constructions like *le loro figlie*, etc., where the pronoun precedes the noun to which it belongs.

---

[1] *loro* has been classed heretofore as a regular conjunctive form, but for the same reason that *noi, voi, lui*, and *lei* are tonic, *loro* is also a tonic form, since it stands after prepositions just as the other forms in *b*.

[2] *Cf.* II, I, 189: Come astolfo *lui* vide in su la sella, A giostra fieramente *lo* sfidava; V, II, 193, se io ucciderò *lui, lo* manderò all' inferno; II, III, 42, Non calse *lei*, ma cavol*la* d'arcione; II, I, 233, Chinque *lei* saluta o *le* favella.

[3] L, p. 203: *ello* suo tempo.

[4] L, p. 209: *ella* guerra.

[5] *Cf.* Biagoli, *Grammaire Italienne*, Paris, 1819, p. 146; Veneroni, *le Maître Italien*, Paris, 1796, p. 105; Abbé Mugnozzi, *Les Élémens de la Langue Italienne*, Paris, 1783, ¶ 144; Fornaciari, *Grammatica Italiana*, Firenze 1891, ¶ 1190.

Syntactical Evolution of *lui, lei, loro.*

Loro (< *illorum*) passes first from the Latin genitive idea to the Italian case of indirect object, being later adopted as the direct object of a verb and subject of a sentence.

The converting of the genitive *loro* into the dative signification is explainad by Schwan[1], who, while treating this form for the French, says: "Die Verwendung des lat. Genitivs zur Bezeichnung eines Dativverhältnisses erklärt sich vielleicht aus dem Gebrauch von *lor-leur* als Possessivum (vgl. ¶ 411, 1). Man sagte z. B. *voi ci lor chastel* und bildete danach *cist chastels lor apartient.*"

The motive that led to the almost universal adoption of the tonic form *loro* in the position of unaccented *gli* and *le* was doubtless a desire to prevent the confusion of these plurals with their singulars of the same form. The change of *lui, lei, loro,* from the dative function to that of the accusative and nominative was perhaps by analogy to *colui, colei, coloro*[2], which were employed as direct object of a verb and subject of a proposition early in the Italian.

The first examples of *lui* and *loro* as nominatives found in the texts on which the present study is based were noted in H., where *loro* occurs ten times as subject and *lui* thirteen times. However, the use of *lui, lei, loro,* as the subject of a verb did not become a regular usage until the time of Manzoni (BBB) in whose works the vernacular of the people plays so important a part.

c.—*me lo,* etc.; *te lo,* etc.; *se lo,* etc.; *me ne, te ne, se ne ;* *glielo,* etc.; *gliene.*

Historical Treatment.

With reference to these double forms Blanc[3] remarks: "Wenn die Pronomina *mi, ti, gli, ci, vi, si,* untereinander verbunden werden, bleiben sie unverändert und getrennt: *mi ti,* mir dich; *ti gli,* dir sie; *vi si,* euch sich; wenn sie aber mit *lo, la, le, li, gli,* und *ne* verbunden werden, so

---

[1] *Grammatik des Altfranzösischen,* ¶ 399, 5 Anm.

[2] *Cf.* Jacomo Cabriele, *Regole Grammaticali,* Venetia, 1545, p. 8 : "Colui, colei, coloro, che dando si a persone più lontane de le primiere, sono dela istessa maniera de le tre dette, nel diritto, e negli obliqui casi parimente ponendosi."

[3] *Grammatik der Italiänischen Sprache,* Halle, 1844, p. 251.

verwandeln sie ihr *i* in *e*. Also nicht *milo, ti la, ci gli, si ne*, sondern *me lo, te lo, ce gli, se ne*, etc." The opinion expressed by this grammarian seems to have been shared by all the Italian grammarians up to his time.

D'Ovidio[1], while discussing these pronouns, says: "Io tengo fermamente, e ho sempre tenuto, che in codeste crasi pronominali l'*e* appartenga al secondo pronome e la vera dissezione sia *m'elo m'ela m'eli m'ele, t'elo* ecc., *s'elo* ecc., *m'ene t'ene s'ene, c'elo* ecc., *v'elo* ecc., *gli' elo* ecc., *gli' ene*."

The double forms included in the quotation above will be considered under the following divisions: Combinations of the first and second person or reflexive with a pronoun of the third person, and combinations of a third personal pronoun with a third person, neither of which is a reflexive.

me lo, etc. ; *te lo*, etc. ; *se lo*, etc. ; *me ne,
te ne, se ne* = *m'ello*, etc. ; *t'ello* etc. ;
s'ello, etc. ; *m'enne, t'enne, s'enne*.

Proving the correctness of the orthography *m'ello*, etc., is, first of all, the preservation of *ello*, etc., and *enne* in the Southern forms *portam-ille, portam-ella, vatt-enne*[2].

Secondly, *elo*, etc., and *ene* for the *ello*, etc., and *enne* in question are still seen in the Tuscan combinations *glielo* (= *gli* + *elo*), *gliela* (= *gli* + *ela*), *gliene* (= *gli* + *ene*)[3]. That this *elo*, etc., and *ene* are survivals of *ello*, etc., and *enne* and that the *e* was not thrown in as a mere glide, when these forms were combined with *gli*, according to Biagoli[4], Mugnozzi[5] and others, is evidenced by the fact that the *e* must have been present before *gli* developed, since this form could have arisen only before a vowel[6].

Thirdly, a similar usage appears in the union of the preposition and article in *dello, nello*, etc., which according to D'Ovidio[7] should be written *d'ello, n'ello*, etc. Here the *i* of *in* and *di* is pretonic and forms an exact parallel to the point in question.

---

[1] Archiv. Glott. It., vol. IV, p. 70, n. 3. Also compare Meyer-Lübke's acceptance of D'Ovidio's theory in his *It. Gr.*, Leipzig, 1890, ¶ 374.

[2] *Cf.* D'Ovidio, *Archiv. Glott. It.*, vol. IV., p. 70, n. 3 ; Meyer-Lübke, It. Gr., ¶ 374.

[3] *Cf.* Meyer-Lübke, *It. Gr.*, ¶ 374.

[4] *Grammaire Italienne*, Paris, 1819, p. 147.

[5] *Les Élémens de la Langue Italienne*, Paris, 1783, ¶ 192.

[6] D'Ovidio, *Glott. It.*, vol. IV., p. 100.

[7] *Archiv. Glott. It.*, vol. IX., p. 70, n. 3.

Thus, from the reasons already given the most logical deduction seems to be to suppose that *me lo*, etc., and *me ne*, etc., were once written *mello*, etc., and *menne*, etc., the *i* being elided before *e*, and, because, in Old Italian the apostrophe was omitted, in the natural process of syllabication the *e* was looked upon as belonging to the *m*, etc., rather than to the *lo*, etc., and *ne*. The writing of *l* and *n* instead of *-ll-* and *-nn-* in these combinations is due to the fact that the two pronouns in *me lo*, etc., and *me ne*, etc., were generally written separate and hence the double consonants could not stand as initial. The probable stages of this development are as follows: *Miello*, etc., *mi enne*, etc. > *mello*, etc.; *menne*, etc. > me *llo*, etc., *me nne*, etc. > *me lo*, etc., *me ne*, etc.

glielo, etc.; *gliela*, etc.; *gliene* = *gliello*, etc., *gliella*, etc., *glienne*.

The original form of these words was probably *gliello*, etc., and *glienne*, this orthography being justified by the fact that the second pronoun in these combinations is tonic, as is shown by the *e* instead of an *i*[1] and hence the writing *gliello*, etc. (< li-illum, etc.) and *glienne* (< li-indĕ) is just as regular as the preservation of the-*ll*-in the nominatives *ello* and *ella*. The reason why Italian writers have always adopted the form with a single *-l-* and *-n-* is doubtless because these forms are analogical growths by the side of *me lo*, etc., where the two pronouns were written separate.

It is to be noted also that in Old as well as in Modern Italian the *gli* in the combinations like *glielo* and *gliene* stands for both masculine *li* and feminine *le*, the *i* of *li* (< illi) remaining and the *e* of *le* becoming *i* regularly in hiatus[2], the result obtained in both cases being *li*, which then > *gli* before the following *e* just as the article *li* > *gli* in *gli amici* (*cf. li elo, le elo* > *li elo* > *glielo*).

Of popular origin are the sporadic occurrences of *gliele*[3] employed for the different forms of *lo* and *la*[4].

---

[1] *Cf.* Meyer-Lübke, *It. Gr.*, ¶ 123.

[2] *Cf.* Meyer-Lübke, *It. Gr.*, ¶ 141.

[3] *Cf.* U, 9, 5: E tutto *gliele* graffiò (il viso); 2, 9, e presentoglicle (i falconi); 2, 8, il conte con lagrime *gliele* diede (la figliuola); 3, 3, piena di stizza *gliele* (a lei) tolsi di mano, ed holla recata a voi, acciocchè voi *gliele* (a lui) rendiate.

[4] *Cf.* Biagoli, *Gram. It.*, Paris, 1819, p. 147; Blanc. *It. Gr.*, p. 252.

d.—The second pronoun in these combinations (No. *c*) is tonic.

In regard to the reason for the change of *i* to *e* in *me lo*, etc., Biagoli[1] remarks: "Ce changement de l' *i* en *e* se fait d'après un principe général d'harmonie, qui exige que lorsqu' un mot sans accent termine en *i*, se joint à un autre mot également privé d'accent, l'on change l' *i* du premier en *e*, sans quoi l' on aurait des mots de deux syllables sans l'accent tonique, ce qui est impossible." Other grammarians who have adopted the writing *me lo*, etc., do not state specifically that the first of these two pronouns is tonic, but merely say that *mi, ti, si* > *me, te, se* when placed before forms like *lo, la, ne*.

With reference to atonic words, Meyer-Lübke[2] posits the following general law: "Il faut tout d'abord remarquer qu' en règle générale il ne peut y avoir deux mots atones de suite, à moins que l'un des deux ne perde sa voyelle: v. g. a.—franç. mel = me-le. Mais habituellement c'est le second, qui est accentué. Par conséquent, les prépositions composées ont toujours l'accent plein: adprópe, ital. apruovo, a.—franç. a pruef."

It is easy to believe that the law just quoted applies to the combinations under discussion, since we naturally lay stress upon the second of the two pronouns; for example, no one ever says *gliélo, gliéne*, but *gliélo, gliéne*.

In the second place, if we accept the conclusions already reached; namely, that *me lo*, etc., should be written *m' ello*, etc.[3], we are forced to admit that, if either of these two forms bear an accent, it must fall upon the second element, since the first loses its vowel in hiatus.

Again, in the parallel combinations formed by the junction of a preposition with a definite article (*cf. d'ello*[4], etc.) the second form is as clearly tonic as are the personal pronouns *ella* and *ello*. Now, since the double forms *d'ello*, etc., and *m'elo* (= *m'ello*) arose under similar conditions; namely, by the union of a monosyllabic atonic with *ello*, etc. (< *illum*), the evidence favoring the accentuation

---

[1] *Grammaire Italienne*, Paris, 1819, p. 60.

[2] *Grammaire des Langues Romanes*, vol. I., ¶ 612.

[3] *Cf.* p. 21.

[4] *Cf.* L, p. 205, *ello* suo tempo; BB, p. 209, *ella* guerra; KK, p. 15, Credette quel *chella* madre diciea; I, p. 11, E 'padre ed *ella* madre.

of the second element of the former would apply equally well to the latter.

The reason why the two *l*'s are preserved in *dello*, etc., and not in *me lo*, etc., is because in the former the two words were generally written as one, while in the latter they were separated, the tonic vowel of the second pronoun being carried to the first, and, hence, the double consonants could not be kept as initial[1].

In the fourth place, if the *ello*, etc., and *enne* in these combinations were not tonic they would have > *illo*, etc., and *inne*[2].

The enclitic uses of *me lo, te lo, se lo, me ne, te ne, se ne, glielo, gliene*, offer no objection to the statement that the second form in the corresponding proclitic combinations is tonic. In constructions like *dirmelo, dirtelo*, the verb being the more important member of the compound retains the stress, while both pronouns are unstressed and hence enclitic according to the rule in Italian that no word can bear more than one tonic accent. However, the *e* is kept in *darmelo*, etc., by analogy to the numerous occurrences of the same combinations in proclitic position.

D.—*Discussion of atonic forms in tonic position.*

1.—Introduced through dialectical influence.

A suggestion offered to explain the substitution of tonic for atonic forms; namely, that they arose from a simple mixing of the two at a time when the laws of syntax were not fixed, might apply here also. However, a most serious objection to this explanation is the fact that the atonic pronouns are not found in the position of the tonic until the time of Boccaccio. If this irregularity is to be attributed to a mere confusion of the unaccented with the accented pronouns, why did it not exist in the earliest Italian monuments, when there was a reason for such a mixing of forms?

A better explanation seems to be to account for this abnormal usage as a borrowing from dialects in which *mi, ti, si* are regular tonic forms.

Strengthening this supposition is the argument that the first occurrences of atonic pronouns in accented position

---
[1] *Cf.* p. 22.
[2] *Cf.* Meyer-Lübke, *It. Gr.*, ¶ 123.

were noted in U[1], where are constantly employed popular forms and idioms. Thus, it is perfectly reasonable to suppose that Boccaccio used *mi* after prepositions under the influence of dialects like the Lombard and Piemontese, and Sacchetti, writing novels of a similar kind, adopted the usage of Boccaccio. Furthermore, the late origin of this construction, the few authors using it, and the long gap between Sacchetti and Goldoni in whose works it is most frequent point to the working of external influences traceable to individual authors rather than to a Tuscan development.

E.—Extent of the mixing of tonic and atonic forms.

By a glance at the table[2] it will be noted that the occurrence of tonic pronouns in atonic position is found in the earliest texts of the language and continues down to a comparatively late date. It will be further observed that, although some authors used them to a much greater extent than others, the usage was a general one and does not seem to have originated with any special class of writers. In addition, it may be said that the line of authors who adopted these irregularities was a continuous one, there being no notable breaks from their origin to their final disappearance, although a very perceptible decrease in their use is observable in the later periods.

The usage of unaccented pronouns in accented position is represented as follows in our texts:

mi, U3, W1, Z6, YY38, FFF; *ti,* YY6.

F.—Time of disappearance.

Me, te, noi, voi, ne, lui and *lei* in proclitic position may be said to have disappeared for the most part from Italian literature before the sixteenth century. *Se* in this position was seldom employed even by the earliest writers and ceased to be used entirely about the fifteenth century. *El* is probably a Provençal[3] form and occurs only in B, K, L, W, AA, CC, YY and can be assigned to no special periods, for the reason that it may be used by any author writing under the influence of this language.

---

[1] Blanc, *It. Gr.*, Halle, 1844, p. 20.
[2] *Cf.* pp. 9-12.
[3] *Cf.* p. 15.

Of the three tonic forms found in enclitic position attached to the verb, *me* was employed until about the time of the Italian Renaissance for the sake of rhyme, while *te* occurs only once[1] and *ne* (meaning "us," "to us") ten times.

In enclitic position not attached to the verb, *me, te, voi, lui, lei* are very frequent in Old Italian, being used sporadically even in the present century; while *noi*, although spread over almost the same period as the forms just mentioned, occurs much less extensively.

The occasional uses of atonics in the position of the accented pronouns are distributed over the long period from Boccaccio to Carducci.

Conclusions.

From the examples and argument given on the preceding pages the following conclusions may be drawn:

1.—That *me, te, se* in proclitic position are remnants of the Latin accusative that had not yet > *mi, ti, si* according to the general law that pretonic $e > i$.

2.—That *el* for *il* was used by certain Tuscan writers through the influence of the Provençal and certain Italian dialects, where this form was the regular oblique masculine singular.

3.—That *me* in enclitic position attached to the verb arose first in rhyme and was later carried to constructions in poetry where it was not used in rhyme[2].

4.—That the *e* of *ne* (< INDE) used for the first person plural is by analogy to *ne* in combinations like *me ne, te ne, se ne* (= *m'enne*, etc.), where the second element is tonic and regularly preserves its *e*. This analogy was carried not only to all the forms of pronominal and adverbial *ne*, but also to the conjunction *ne*.

5.—That *noi, voi, lui, lei, loro* in proclitic and enclitic position are a simple application or development of tonic pronouns in unaccented position. The change of *loro* from the genitive to the dative function was by analogy to possessive constructions, like *la loro casa* on which was built the kindred idea expressed by *la casa loro appartiéne*. The further evolution of *lui, lei, loro* from the sphere of

---

[1] *Cf.* DD, p. 181.

[2] *Te* occurs only once joined to the verb (*cf.* DD, p. 181).

the dative to that of the accusative and nominative is by analogy to *colui, colei, coloro*.

6.—That *me lo*, etc.; *te lo*, etc.; *se lo*, etc.; *me ne*, etc., should be written *m'ello*, etc., and that the reason why these forms are written with a single *l* at present is because the tonic vowel of the second pronoun has been transferred to the first and the two *l*'s cannot stand as initial (*cf. me llo > me lo*).

7.—That *glielo*, etc., and *gliene* are equivalent to *gliello*, etc., and *glienne*, one *l* being omitted in modern orthography by analogy to the parallel combinations *me lo*, etc. Also, the *gli* in these double forms is the representative of masculine *li* (< ILLI) and feminine *le* (< ILLAE), both giving *gli* in hiatus with the *e* of the following word (*cf. li ene, le ene > gliene*).

8.—That the second form in the combinations *m'ello*, etc., and *gliello*, etc., is tonic.

9.—That the use of atonic *mi* and *ti* in accented position is due to the influence of dialects in which these forms are regular tonic developments.

CHAPTER II.

Uses of Atonic Forms in Atonic Position.

A.—Examples of regular occurrences in texts examined.

THE pronouns indicated below comply with all the conditions of atonics, showing unaccented forms and standing in conjunctive position, and are therefore perfectly regular. After an example of each phenomenon has been given, a discussion of these pronouns will be taken up.

1.—General Constructions.

The list of occurrences mentioned below represents the usage common to all the periods of the Italian language, and hence merely an example of each kind will be cited, and no résumé will follow. They include especially proclitic[1] constructions of the direct and indirect object of finite verbs where the adoption of atonic pronouns is the rule, with the exception of the occasional use of tonic[2] forms immediately before the verb, or atonics as enclitics[3], which special uses have already been counted[4].

a.—Single proclitics.
aa.—*Before finite verbs.*

mi : GG, p. 80,
    Questo *mi* prese, e questo *mi* mantenne.
mi[5] : BBB, p. 16,
    mi dispiace.
ci : O, Purg. XV, 104,
    Che farem noi a chi ne desira,
    Se quei che *ci* ama e per noi condannato ?

---

[1] *Cf. lo* menò, *mi* parlò.

[2] *Cf. lui* menò ; *me* parlò.

[3] *Cf.* menòllo ; parlòmmi.

[4] *Cf.* résumé of tonic forms in proclitic position, pp. 9-10 also résumé of enclitics with finite verbs, pp. 41-42.

[5] The dative will follow the accusative wherever the two constructions are given.

ci: II, I, 94,
  Molte comodità *ci* ha date Iddio
  Per ricompensa de le nostre pene.
ti: O, Inf. I, 123,
  Con lei *ti* lascerò nel mio partire.
ti: II, I, 120,
  non *ti* converrà morire.
vi: Z, I, nov. 4,
  dice all'Abate: io *vi* caverò di questa fatica.
vi: O, Inf. XXIII, 128,
  Poscia drizzò al frate cotal voce:
  Non *vi* dispiaccia, se *vi* lece, dirci
  Se alla man destra giace alcuna foce.
si sing.: BB, p. 65,
  E Carduin da lei non *si* diparte.
si plu.: FFF, Ode Barbare, p. 23,
  poi *si* riabbracciano.
lo after a final consonant: O, Purg. IX, 81,
  E come l'occhio più e più v'apersi
  Vidil seder sopra il grado soprano,
  Tal nella faccia, ch'io non *lo* soffersi.
lo before *s* impure: O, Inf. I, 110,
  Noi leggevamo un giorno per diletto
  Di Lancilotto, come amor *lo* strinse.
la: O, Inf. I, 109,
  Questi *la* caccerà per ogni villa.
le: II, I, 82,
  Ma così nudo e furfante ed a piede,
  Fa cose da non creder chi *le* vede.
le: U, 2, 6,
  li quali *le* parevano la più dolce cosa del mondo.

bb.—Before infinitive constructions.

1. Negative infinitives used imperatively:
  AAA, I, p. 132, non *ti* turbare.
2. Infinitives depending on impersonal verbs:
  B, p. 27, ma non *mi* val seguire.
3. Infinitives depending on *fare, vedere, sentire, udire, lasciare*:
  A, p. 90 v, Amor d'incontra *mi* fa star sospeso.

b.—Single enclitics.

aa.—*Attached to infinitives*[1].

1. With subject infinitive : U, I, 1,
    il mandar*lo* fuori di casa nostra così
    infermo ne sarebbe gran biasimo.
2. With infinitive depending on noun : S, p. 330,
    Turno ha intendimento di cacciar*mi*.
3. With infinitive depending on adjective : U, 5, 8,
    io son presto di far*lo*.
4. With object infinitive preceded by *di* : S, p. 291,
    desideriava di dar*la*.
5. With purpose infinitives preceded by *per* : S, p. 22,
    li artisani li loro artifici lasciavano per veder*lo*.
6. With infinitive depending directly on transitive verbs[2] :
    U, 9, 5, pensa voler*lo* onorare.

bb.—*Attached to imperatives.*

1. With the first person plural imperative :
    FFF, Studi Lett., p. 251, e traduciamo*la* con qualche commento.
2. With the imperative second singular and plural :
    F, p. 27, disse : di*mi*, di*mi* e insegna*mi* che chosa, e la prudenza :
    BBB, p. 6, inseguite*mi*.
3. With *ecco* : II, I, 43,
    ecco*li* insieme.

c.—Constructions common to proclitic and enclitic position.

1. Indirect object with verbs accompanied by *innanzi, dietro, sopra, dirempetto, incontra, davanti, avanti, incontro, dentro, dinanzi* :
    V, II, 208, *gli* venne incontra.
2. Dative strengthening the possessive : H, p. 195,
    lo Cardinale *si* levò lo capello.

---

[1] For the use of pronouns with the present participle compare F. p. 50 : Mostrando*mi* li pericoli.

[2] Except verbs of making, causing, seeing, feeling, hearing, letting, permitting.

3. Active reflexive in which the agent is the voluntary cause of the action:
F, p. 21, alora *si* levò l'uno de'medici di fedite.
4. Passive reflexive in which the agent suffers the action without willing it: K, p. 21,
O figliuolo mio, perchè *ti* spaventi tue di tanta paura?
5. First person precedes the second: O, Par. VIII, 52,
La mia letizia *mi ti* tien celato.-
6. First and second persons precede the reflexive *si*:
F, p. 53, non *ti si* scuopra lo lato.

2.—SPECIAL CONSTRUCTIONS.

In addition to rare uses, idiomatic phrases, speech formulas and locutions, the following examples include mainly those constructions which belong more especially to individual writers in certain epochs rather than to the Italian language as a whole.

a.—Single proclitics.

Nominatives.

i': O, Inf. I, 8,
Ma per trattar del ben ch'*i'* vi trovai,
Dirò dell'altre cose ch'io v'ho scorte;
Inf. X, 34,
I'aveva già il mio viso nel suo fitto.

no': O, Purg. V, 52 (Blanc, It. Gr. p. 255),
No' fummo già tutti per forza morti;
PP, p. 77
Qui *no'* siam soli, e so' d'opinione
Che la si volterà in poche parole.

vo'[1]: N, p. 76,
k'avemo scritte dolorosamente
quelle parole ke *vo'* avete udite;
N, p. 17,
ch' i' dissi lor: *vo'* portate le chiave
di ciascuna vertù alta e gentile.

e': II, I, 26,
Rispose Ferraguto: *e'* mi da 'l core;
O, Inf. XXII, 101,
Sì ch' *e'* non teman delle lor vendetta.

---

[1] X, p. 17; TT, pp. 82, 169, 174.

gli[1]: TT, p. 130,
>Gli è cittadino, e noi zappiam la terra
>TT, p. 72,
>Gli è un che va vestito di cilesto.

la[2]: EE, p. 264,
>La non vuol esser più mia,
>La non vuol la traditora,
>L' è disposta al più ch'io muora
>Per amor, e gelosia.

l'[3] = *la*: PP, p. 85,
>E l' altanto più che la mie manza,
>Poi che la sa che *l'* è tenuta bella.

gli plu.[4]: TT, p. 83,
>Insino a ora, i' n' ho gettati motti:
>Gli han fatto il sordo, e sono stati chiotti;
>TT, p. 169,
>Gli han fatto visi che pajon la morte.

le[5]: KK, II, 305,
>sebbene le cose sono in superlativo grado tutto bene, subito *le si* convertono in un pessimo male
>TT, p. 124,
>*le* son pur cose ladre.

Atonic forms in hiatus.

mi[6]: O, Inf. V, 105,
>Amor, che a nullo amato amar perdona,
>Mi prese del costui piacer sì forte,
>Che, come vedi, ancor non *mi* abbandona.

m'[7]: O, Inf. I, 20,
>Allor fu la paura un poco queta,
>Che nel lago del cor *m'*era durata
>La notte, ch' i' passai con tanta pieta.

---

[1] *Cf.* PP, p. 70; FF, pp. 8r, 55r, 23r; TT, pp. 121, 129, 166, 181.

[2] This form occurs twelve times as nominative in EE, p. 264.

[3] *Cf.* PP, p. 75; TT, pp. 93, 99, 149; KK, II, 333.

[4] *Cf.* W, Ar, Cv, &iiir; MM, pp. 59, 114.

[5] *Cf.* TT, pp. 86, 82, 121; KK, I, 407, II, 292; U, 2, 9; 8, 3; V, II, 80; AA, p. 83; GG, p. 429; MM, pp. 52, 58, 59, 73, 80, 96, 105.

[6] Wherever the vowel that follows the atonic form written is not mentioned, the form given is found equally before all vowels.

[7] The pronoun eliding its vowel will be placed immediately under the one written in full.

ci^1 before *e* or i^2: U, 1, 1,
    faccendo noi nostro mezzano un suo nemico, amico
    credendolo, *ci* exaudisce, come se ad uno vera-
    mente santo per mezzano della sua gratia ricor-
    resimo.

c' before e^3 or *i*: O, Inf. XII, 51,
    O cieca cupidigia, e ria e folle,
    Che si ci sproni nella vita corta,
    E nell' eterna poi si mal *c'*immolle.

ti: K, I, 77,
    non *ti* ho mai veduto pigliare.

t': K, I, 176,
    di chi *t'* ha fatto male.

vi: O, Par. XXX, 139,
    La cieca cupidigia, che *vi* ammalia,
    Simili fatti *v'* ha al fantolino,
    Che muor di fame e caccia via la balia.

v': J, p. 18,
    noi *v'* entendaremo.

si: O, Inf. I, 100,
    Molti son gli animali a cui *si* ammoglia.

s': BB, p. 38,
    E'nverso lui ella *s'* affoltava.

lo: O, Purg. XIV, 69,
    Come all'annunzio de' dogliosi danni
    Si turba il viso di colui che ascolta,
    Da qual che parte il periglio *lo* assanni.

l': J, p. 15,
    tu ce *l'* ài mandato.

la: VV, p. 93,
    ma che il mare statole poco
    propizio ne *la* avesse divertita.

l': Y, nov. 13,
    l' avea tanto veduta.

le dat. fem. sing.: LL, I, 231,
    Così dicea la donna con gran pianto,
    Quando *le* apparve l'eremita accanto.

---

[1] Before *a*, *o* and *u*, *ci* is not elided.
[2] *Cf.* K, I, 234.
[3] *Cf.* K, I, 144.

l' dat. fem. sing.: LL, I, 21,
>Non risponde ella, e non sa che si faccia
>Perchè Rinaldo omai *l'*è troppo appresso.

Il, 'l, lo after a final vowel and before a single consonant.

Il: O, Inf. II, 31,
>........chi *il* concede ?
>Inf. V, 110, Chinai il viso, e tanto *il* tenni basso.

'l: O, Purg. I, 39, io *'l* vedea.

lo: II, I, 8, In viso Balagante *lo* guardava;
>O, Inf. VIII, 41, Per che il maestro accorto *lo* sospinse.

il[1] and *lo*[2] equivalent to English *so* or *it*:
>WW, p. 259, Arminsi pure i Greci,
>>Furo ingrati ad Achille, e *il* sieno a Pirro;
>
>YY, X, 243, *il* sarete.—
>WW, p. 267, Ei giurerà d'esser sostegno al figlio,
>>E *lo* sarà ecc.;
>
>YY, I, 58,.......sarò padre
>>Per compiacerti, come ora *lo* sono
>>Per consigliarti.

i accu. plu.[3]: O, Inf. V, 78,
>Ed egli a me: " vedrai quando saranno
>Più presso a noi; e tu allor li prega
>Per quell'amor che *i* mena; e quei verranno;'
>
>Inf. VII, 53,
>La sconoscente vita, che *i* fe' sozzi,
>Ad ogni conoscenza or li fa bruni.

i indirect singular[4]: O, Par. XXIV, 148,
>Come il signor ch'ascolta quel che *i* piace,
>Da indi abbraccia il servo, gratulando
>Per la novella, tosto ch'ei si tace;
>
>O, Par, XXIX, 17,
>In sua eternità di tempo fuore,
>Fuor d'ogni altro comprender, come *i* piacque,
>S'aperse in nuovi amor l'eterno amore.

---

[1] *Cf.* WW, p. 255.
[2] *Cf.* WW, p. 256; ZZ, XIII, 276, 120; BBB, pp. 125, 263.
[3] *Cf.* O, Inf. XVIII, 18, Par. XII, 26; J, p. 3.
[4] *Cf.* O, Inf. XXII, 73: Inf. XXII, 127.

Dative of the possessor[1]: WW, p. 260,
   gli sarò padre;
AAA, VI, 68,
   non ti son figlio io primo?
gli fem. dat. sing.: U, 2, 6,
   li quali le parevano la più dolce cosa del mondo et la più vezzosa, et non essendolesi anchora del nuovo parto rasciuto il latte del petto quelli teneramente prese, et al petto *gli* si puose, li quali non rifiutando il servigio, così lei peppavano, come la madre havrebber fatto;
O, Inf. XXXIII, 129 (Blanc, *It. Gr.* p. 263).
   Sappi che tosto che l'anima trade,
   Come fec'io, il corpo suo *gli* è tolto.

b.—Single enclitics with finite verbs[2].

mi: N, p. 25,
   menòm*mi* sott'una freschetta folgla;
Z, nov. 4,
   e raderòm*mi* la barba.
ci: O, Inf. VI, 23,
   Quando ci scorse Cerbero, il gran vermo,
   Le bocche aperse, e mostròc*ci* le sanne.
Inf. IV, 115,
   Traemmo*ci* dall'un de'canti
   In loco aperto luminoso ed alto,
   Sì che veder poteansi tutti e quanti.
ti: U, 6, 6,
   et havròt*ti* in reverenza;
U, 2, 5,
   dico*ti*, che poi che Iddio mi ha fatto tanta gratia.
vi: P, I, 14,
   Prego*vi*, siate accorti.
si: O, Inf. IV, 98,
   volser*si* a me.

---

[1] *Cf.* DD, p. 134; TT, p. 104; WW, p. 266; AAA, I, 146, 161, 175.

[2] Examples of the first and second person imperative are not given in this list because the unaccented pronouns are still attached to this mode in the persons indicated.

lo: B, p. 43,
    Ma pur la fine facie*lo* laudato;
  B, p. 43,
    E poi nel mezo avete*lo* sequito,
    Lo bon fenir vi de' essere in grato.

l: P, I, 59,
    E mis*il* per la via quasi smarrita ;
  P, II, 6,
    Vede*l* colei, ch' è or si presso al vero.

la: O, Inf. XVIII, 94,
    Lasciò*lla* quivi gravida e soletta ;
  M, nov. 12,
    combatteo la città, e vinsc*la*, e lo pregio e l'onore
    n'ebbe David.

li[1] *:* F, p. 68,
    prese*li* a pregare ;
  p. 56,
    concede*li* di peccare.

gli : O, Purg. XIII, 153,
    Tu li vedrai tra quella gente vana
    Che spera in Talamone, e perdera*gli*
    Più di speranza, che a trovar la Diana ;
  O, Inf. XXII, 71,
    E Libicocco: Troppo avem sofferto,
    Disse, e prese*gli* il braccio col ronciglio,
    Sì che, stracciando, ne portò un lacerto.

le: V, I, 15,
    cominciò*lle* a mostrare e veli e borse;
  O, Inf. V, 68,
    Vidi Paris, Tristano ; e più di mille
    Ombre mostrommi e nomino*lle* a dito.

c.—Enclitics with *che, dietro, addosso, dreto.*

mi with *che*[2] *:* N, p. 20,
    questi è colui, che*mmi* si fa sentire.

---

[1] Since case and number offer no assistance in the explanation of enclitics, no distinction has been made between the singular and plural, or dative and accusative of *li* and *gli*.

[2] *Cf.* N, pp. 25, 32.

mi with *dietro*: KK, II, 70,
    loro sempre venivano a lento passo
    dietro*mi*;
        KK, II, 175,
    deretro*mi*.

gli with *addosso*: KK, I, 114,
    e'l cavallo addosso*gli*;
        KK, I, 271,
    eglino tutti l'un sopra all'altro addosso*gli*.

gli with *drieto*: Z, nov. 70,
    l'altro porco drieto*gli*;
        Z, nov. 76,
    gli fanciulli con le granate
    drieto*gli*.

li with *drieto*: Z, nov. 84,
    mino, drieto*li* parecchi passi gridava;
        I, p. 6,
    elleno dietro*li* co' bastoni.

d.—Constructions common to proclitic and enclitic position.

vi = *le*: EEE, p. 274,
    voleva la neve, camminar*vi* sopra.

vi = *gli*: BBB, p. 6,
    non potendo schivare il pericolo,
    vi corse incontro.

la, indefinite[1]: BBB, 384,
    cominciò a prenderse*la* con Perpetua;
        DDD, p. 14,
    dunque, a che serve pigliarse*la* a cuore?

l' = la indefinite: BBB, p. 65,
    l' è chiara, che l'intenderebbe ognuno;
        BBB, p. 130,
    "*L'*è dura," rispose il Griso, restando con un piede sul primo scalino, "*l'* è dura di ricever de' rimproveri, dopo aver lavorato fedelmente."

---

[1] *Cf*. BBB, pp. 209, 282 (four *l*mes), 232; DDD, pp. 112, 145.

Pronouns of address.

vi, to princes: KK, II, 202,
   ora ascoltatemi, Ser Francesco Riccio, che io *vi* dirò
   che sono i mia pari;
KK, II, 234,
   Vostra Eccellenza non diffidi di me; il perchè di
   nuovo le dico, che a me basta la vista di condurre
   tre volte meglio quest' opera, che non fu il
   modello; siccome io *v'* ho promesso.

la: KK, II, 316,
   majordomo insinoattanto che Vostra Signoria parlerà secondo quel nobilissimo grado, in che ella e
   in volta, io *la* riverirò e parlerò a lei con quella
   sommessione, io l' ho da servire;
KK, II, 195,
   e perchè sua eccellenza vedessi quanto io avevo
   voglia di servir*la*.

le: KK, II, 234,
   Vostra Eccellenza non diffidi di me; il perchè di
   nuovo *le* dico, che a me basta la vista di condurre
   tre volte meglio quest'opera, che non fu il modello.

ella: KK, II, 238,
   sappi l'Eccellenza Vostra, che le ribalderie di Bernardone mi sforzano a dimandarla e pregarla, che
   quella mi dica quel ch'*ella* spesse nel diamante,
   grande punta ischericata; perchè io spero mostrarle, perche questo mal cerca mettermivi in disgrazia.

e.—Double atonics in which the direct precedes the indirect object in combinations where *mi, ti, ci, vi*
   stand next to *lo*, etc., *la*, etc.

il before *mi*[1]: U, 7, 9,
   ella *il mi* comanderà;
   U, 3, 7,
   se voi il sapete, dite*lmi*.

la before *mi*[2]: U, 6, 4,
   in fe di Dio se tu non *la mi* dai;

---
[1] U, 5, 9; 7, 7; 10, 10; 8, 7; 8, 7; 8, 8; O, *Inf.* XXV, 48; O, *Inf.* XVI, 44; *Par.* XXV, 89.
[2] U, 3, 1; 2, 10; 3, 9; 7, 10; 5, 1; 5, 4; 8, 8.

> U, 2, 10,
> ove così non fosse voi foreste villania a voler*lami* torre.

il before *ti*[1] : U, 5, 4,
> io *il ti* prometto ;
> U, 5, 10,
> tien*loti* a mente.

la before *ti*[2] : U, 3, 4,
> io *la ti* mosterrò ;
> U, 4, 4,
> noi *la ti* diamo.

il before *vi*[3] : U, 1, 1,
> io *il vi* dirò ;
> U, 6, 10,
> dirò*lvi*.

la before *vi*[4] : U, 3, 6,
> hora non credo io, che voi crediate, che io *la vi* mandossi ;
> U, 2, 9,
> ma se le vi piacciono, io *le vi* donerò volentieri.

B.—RÉSUMÉ.

The following table gives a résumé of the examples of the special constructions cited above.

a.—Single proclitics.
Atonic Nominatives.

> *i'* : B31, C, F9, H3, K2, M3, N46, O24, P361, R6, S2, U3, V11, W8, X19, Y2, AA30, BB39, DD88, EE8, FF9, GG51, HH10, II18, JJ, KK, LL2, NN5, PP81, QQ72, SS114, TT148, UU6, XX17.
>
> *no'* : D2, X, PP, TT12, O.
>
> *vo'* : N2, X, TT3.

---

[1] *Cf.* U, 7, 9 ; 9, 5 ; O, *Inf.* III, 45 ; O, *Purg.* XX, 40 ; *Purg.* XXXIII, 77 ; *Purg.* XXXIII, 119.
[2] *Cf.* U, 3, 14 ; 5, 2 ; 8, 7 ; 10, 3.
[3] *Cf.* U, 3, 3 ; 3, 7 ; 3, 7 ; 8, 9 ; 9, 1 ; O, Par. XIV, 10.
[4] *Cf.* U, 3, 6 ; 5, 1.

e': B7, C2, F9, H10, I2, K10, M2, N6, O13, P18, R7, S2, U2, V117, X4, Y16, Z154, AA3, BB43, DD4, EE2, GG68, HH2, II33, KK316, LL, MM2, NN4, PP9, QQ5, RR3, SS3, TT174, XX, DDD5, EEE, FFF26.

gli sing.: W, FF3, LL13, PP, QQ, TT53, YY2, DDD10.

gli plu.: W6, TT2, MM2.

la: EE12, II7, KK19, LL, MM11, PP7, TT79, YY38, BBB19, DDD5.

l' = la: AA, PP2, TT34, KK, BBB6, DDD4.

le: U2, V, AA, GG, KK7, MM8, TT10, BBB6, DDD.

Proportion of forms not elided when *mi, ti, si, vi, lo, la,* and the feminine plural *le* are placed in hiatus[1].

KK²40%, VV75%, WW25%, YY22%, ZZ28%, AAA (vol. VI.) 38%, DDD22%, EEE80%, FFF28%[3].

il, 'l, lo following a final vowel and preceding a single consonant initial.

il: A2, B9, C3, E, H, I4, K6, M31, O72, P48, K11, S2, U455, V18, W4, X3, Y9, Z40, AA11, BB8, CC8, DD4, EE5, FF7, GG24, HH6, II260, LL141, MM3, NN26, OO15, PP, QQ62, RR, SS42, TT6, UU42, WW29, XX22, YY5, ZZ4, AAA90, CCC16.

'l: A, B9, C5, E, F4, K8, M16, N8, O6, P71, R17, S7, U23, V10, X4, Y, Z3, AA5, BB6, DD10, EE6, FF5, GG16, II27, LL32, NN2, OO13, PP5, QQ25, SS31, TT14, UU18, WW3, XX12, YY3, AAA23.

---

[1] *Ci* is subject to the same laws of elision as *mi*, etc., when it occurs before the vowels *e* and *i*, but it is always written in full before *a, o* and *u*.

[2] The percentage of elision in each author may easily be computed by subtracting the numerals placed to the right of the capital letters from a hundred.

[3] In all the texts not mentioned the proportion of non-elision is less than 2%.

lo: A5, B43, C8, E7, F8, H20, I10, K53, M30, N4, O13, S126, U9, V162, W15, X, Y98, Z160, AA5, BB9, CC3, DD5, EE12, FF14, GG44, HH, II369, LL541, MM54, NN13, OO8, PP4, RR2, SS4, TT27, UU23, VV17, WW23, XX8, YY90, ZZ69, AAA7, CCC2.

il and *lo* equivalent to English *so*.
il: WW2, AAA4.
lo: WW3, YY, AAA2.
i accusative plural: J, O4.
i dative singular: O5, N2.
gli fem. dative singular: O, U.
Dative of the possessor: DD, TT, WW2, YY, AAA3.

b.—Single enclitics.
With finite verbs[1].

mi: A4, B23, C2, E8, F, K3, M2, N3, O94, P4, R3, S2, T3, U53, V13, W19, X4, Y4, Z18, AA2, BB3, CC9, DD18, EE, FF10, GG29, II19, JJ6, KK37, LL2, MM, NN5, OO4, PP5, QQ4, SS13, TT5, AA, WW3, XX13, YY16, ZZ3, AAA15, CCC, FFF4.
ci: O6, R4, U2, DD, GG2, JJ, KK, AAA.
ti: K, M3, O3, R4, S2, U8, W2, X, Z10, DD, GG4, II2, KK, LL, NN, OO2, SS, XX, YY, AAA8.
vi: B6, C, E, O, P5, S2, U10, BB2, II5, KK, XX, YY, AAA.
si[2]: I, Y2, II, FFF2.
lo: B9, G, H27, I10, K26, L, M31, O9, P6, R, S18, T9, U39, V22, W4, X, Y, Z49, BB5, DD4, FF2, GG2, II30, JJ6, KK3, LL42, MM2, NN2, OO, PP, QQ4, SS4, TT, UU5, XX6, YY, CCC4, DDD, FFF.

[1] The first and second person imperative are excluded from this résumé because the atonics are still attached to this mode in the persons mentioned.

[2] This résumé includes only the reflexive *si* and not the uses of this form as a sign of the passive signification of the verb.

l : A, B2, E, O4, P4, R, U3, W2, BB3, I I3, SS3, TT, AAA.

la : A, B, C, F, H3, I, K4, M10, N, O4, P3, S, T4, U8, V16, Y2, Z14, EE3, GG, II6, JJ2, KK, LL21, MM, NN3, OO, PP, QQ3, TT4, WW2, XX4, AAA3, BBB, FFF2.

li : B2, F2, G2, H6, I4, K7, L3, M56, O5, R, S13, T8, V4, W2, Y10, Z17, AA, GG6, II2, KK, LL3, MM, SS3, WW.

gli : D, H9, I4, O7, P2, S7, T, U81, V40, W5, Z70, BB11, EE3, FF8, GG8, II80, JJ2, KK5, LL35, NN3, QQ4, TT, UU3, VV, XX2, AAA, CCC5, FFF.

le : C, E, I, K5, M8, O2, P2, U13, V16, W, Z, II3, JJ, KK, TT, XX, FFF.

Atonics with *che, dereto, drieto, addosso.*
mi with *che:* N8.
mi with *dereto:* KK.
mi with *drieto:* KK.
gli with *drieto:* Z.
gli with *addosso:* KK2.
li with *drieto:* I, Z2.

c.—*Constructions common to proclitic and enclitic position.*

vi equivalent to a third personal dative : II, BBB, EEE.

la and *l'* (= *la*) used indefinitely.
la : BBB13, DDD3 ; *l'* : BBB4.

d. Pronouns of address.

In order to show the relative frequency of the mixing and competing constructions of *voi* and *ella* the corresponding tonic pronouns will be placed to the right of the unaccented forms. In the texts not included in this résumé, *voi* is adopted, to the exclusion of *ella*, as the form of polite address.

vi : KK18, YY205. | *voi* : KK13, YY162.
la : KK14, RR, YY12, BBB13, DDD. | *ella* : KK16, RR4, VV, YY11, BBB.
le : V, KK4, RR5, VV2, YY4, BBB46, DDD5. | *lei* : KK3, RR6, VV3, YY3, BBB124, DDD33.

e.—Double atonics in which the direct precedes the indirect object[1].

il mi : B3, E, M4, O, P, U6, W, NN, SS.
lo mi : B, M2, O, U4, BB, LL, NN, FFF.
la mi : B, U7, KK, NN3, OO, PP, TT.
le mi : P, U3, NN2.
il ci : M, U.
lo ci : U, NN.
le ci : NN.
il ti : O5, U3, SS.
lo ti : B, M2, O3, U, Z, NN2, UU.
la ti : M2, N, U4, NN2.
le ti : UU.
il vi : U20, NN.
lo vi : C, M4, O.
la vi : U2, NN2.
le vi : U3, NN.

C.—Discussion of single atonics.

1.—In proclitic position.
a.—Nominatives *i'*, *i*, *no'*, *vo'*, *e'*, *gli*, *la*, *l'* (= *la*), *le*.

On this point Meyer-Lübke[2] remarks : " Im Toskanischen kennt von Subjektivepronomina nur *io* eine proklitische Form : *i*, die in alter Zeit auch in der Litteratur gebräuchlich war, s. Caix, Orig. 210."

---
[1] This table includes only combinations of the first and second personal forms with a third person not reflexive.
[2] *Cf. It. Gr.*, ¶ 369.

Of the other proclitic[1] forms above mentioned *e'*[*] certainly points, because of the frequency of its occurrence in the best Italian texts[2] to a Tuscan origin and growth, just as in the case of *i'* and *i;* while the shortened nominatives *no'*[4], *vo'*[5], *gli'*[6], *la'*[7], *l'* (= la) and *le* belong more especially to popular speech[8].

E'[9] the elided form of *ei* can stand only before a consonant, while *i'*[10] and *i*[11], the shortened forms of *io* are used both before vowels and consonants.

Interesting as a study of the Italian folk speech is the use of double nominatives[12] in cases where a noun standing as the regular subject of a proposition is followed by a pronoun used as the subject of the same verb[13]. Illustrating a similar usage is the occurrence of two objects[14] after

[1] *Cf.* Caix, *Origini*. Firenze, 1880, ¶ 91 : "Come casi d'iato all'atona vanno qui considerate le forme apostrofate delle enclitiche e proclitiche e particolarmente dei pronomi personali *eo, io, noi, voi, lei,* e dei possessivi *meo, mio, tuo, suo;* onde abbiamo : *e', i', no', vo', le', me', mi', tu', su'.*"
Also compare Fornaciari, *Grammatica Italiana*. Firenze 1879, p. 120 :
Proclitiche : gli ed e' = egli, eglino,
la = ella,
le = elleno.

[2] *Cf.* Caix, *Origini*, ¶ 91 : "Questa ci conduce poi alle forme *ei, quei, e', que',* principalmente toscane, e frequenti già in Guittone e nella sua Scuola."

[3] *Cf.* résumé, p. 39.

[4] *Cf.* Caix, *Origini*, ¶ 207.

[5] *vo'* occurs also in the oblique cases in K, pp. 27, 35, 42, 46, 61, 116 ; N, p. 43.

[6] *Cf.* the 44 occurrences of *gli* in the popular writer TT by the side of the seventy-nine examples of the vulgar nominative *la* in the same text.

[7] *Cf.* Blanc, *It. Gr.*, p. 272 : "Jetzt ist der Gebrauch der, dass *ella* und *elleno* der edleren Sprache, *la* und *elle* dem gewöhnlichen Leben, *le* aber fur *elleno* nur dem Pöbel angehört."

[8] For examples of all the atonic nominatives cited above, compare pp. 31-32.

[9] *Cf.* V, I, 10 : *E'* non vide mai nessuno compiuto.

[10] *Cf.* DD, p. 5 : *l'* era divenuto tanto stanco ;
LL, I, 232, Padre, di me ch' i' son giunta a mal porto.

[11] *Cf.* Blanc, *It. Gr.*, p. 95 : "Auch der Apostroph ist im Italiänischen eine neuere Erfindung, die Handschriften des 14. Jahrh. kennen ihn nicht."

[12] *Cf.* KK, I, 407 : Questa *prigione*, che certo innocentissimo tu hai avuta, *la* sarà stata la salute per sempre.

[13] *Cf.* Henry, *he* is going to town to-morrow, a usage common among English peasants.

[14] *Cf.* KK, II, 1 : Questo capitolo *lo* scrivo a Luca Martini.

one verb in which the second is a pronoun inserted after the regular noun object.

b.—Atonic pronouns in hiatus[1].

The general law governing the elision or retention of the final vowel of the pronominal and adverbial particles in hiatus is that *mi*[2], *ti*, *si*, *ne*, *vi*, *lo*, *la* are generally elided when placed before any vowel or *h*, while *ci* loses its vowel only when standing before *i*[3] or *e*, and it is written in full before *a*[4], *o* and *u*. The *i* of *gli*[5], singular and plural, is elided only before an initial *i;* and the *e* of *le*[6] (the accusative feminine plural) is cut off before another *e* provided the context is sufficiently clear to prevent the confusion of *le* (the plural form) with *le*, the dative singular.

The rules, as given, are those generally practised from the origin of the language to the latest writers. However, there are found in the usage of certain authors striking exceptions to the laws postulated, which exceptions render necessary a comparison of the different texts studied. In the course of this examination[7] I have noted that the elision of atonic particles was general until about the sixteenth century, from which time the proportion of non-elided forms rapidly increases, reaching the greatest percentage in VV, AAA, EEE, DDD, FFF, etc., where the use of a full or shortened form is optional[8].

2.—In enclitic position.

a.—Origin of *mi*, *ti*, *si*.

With reference to the origin of the use of *mi, ti, si* as enclitics, D'Ovidio[9] says: " Nulla però ci vieta di supporre che, sorti nella posizione proclitica, *mi* ecc. passassero quindi anche alla enclitica." While this development may

---

[1] The adverbs *ci*, *ne* and *vi* are also included in the present treatment of elision.

[2] *Cf.* m'amò ; t'offendere ; n'andò ; v'ha amato : l'ha veduto.

[3] *Cf.* c'insegna ; c'entra.

[4] *Cf.* ci amò ; ci offese ; ci udiva.

[5] *Cf.* gl'indusse ; gli amò.

[6] *Cf.* l'ebbe trovate.

[7] *Cf.* table p. 40.

[8] *Cf.* examples pp. 32-33.

[9] *Archiv. Glott. It.*, vol. IX., p. 70.

be possible, one is led to reject it for the reason that the pronouns in hand can be explained on a purely phonetic basis.

According to a general phonetic law given by Meyer-Lübke:[1] "Dagegen wird *ē* zu *i: fiori, ami = amēs, chimenti, Giovanni, oggi - hodie, vedi = vidē,*" *mē*, etc., regularly > *mi*, etc., in postonic position.

The junction of enclitic pronouns with the verbs upon which they lean is simply an orthographic representation of the sounds of oral speech; the two words being articulated together, orthography in attempting to indicate pronunciation writes the two forms as one.

3. Constructions common to proclitic and enclitic position (or partly proclitic and partly enclitic).

a.—Mixing of gender, number and person.

aa.—Masculine for feminine.

The occasional use of masculine *gli*[2] for the indirect feminine singular *le* (< P. L.[3] ILLAE) is best explained as deriving directly < ILLI (= C. L. masc. and fem. dat. sing.). Since the Latin shows both ILLI and ILLAE for the feminine dative singular, it is natural that *gli* and *le*, their respective derivatives, should persist side by side until the former is supplanted by *le*, the Italian representative of the latter.

An apparent confusion of gender may be seen in the sporadic use of the oblique masculine singular *lo*[4] for *la*, where the masculine form merely expresses some quality of the feminine noun to which it refers, but does not stand in the place of the noun in the ordinary sense of a pronoun.

Forming a striking contrast to the mixing of gender just referred to, is the strict preservation of the feminine in elliptical and indefinite constructions; such as, *vedersela, pagarla, godersela*[5], etc., where the verb is accompanied by a pronoun without relating to anything before mentioned.

---

[1] *It. Gr.*, ¶ 106.

[2] *Cf.* p. 35.

[3] P. L. = Popular Latin and C. L. = Classic Latin.

[4] *Cf.* BBB, p. 125: Gertrude avrebbe potuto essere una monaca santa e contenta, comunque *lo* fosse divenuta.

[5] *Cf.* The French "*vous me la donnez belle*" and the Spanish "*quien las sabe las tañe.*"

In such idiomatic expressions, although some substantive is always understood, agreeing with the sense to which the pronoun refers[1], there would seem to be a natural reason for a mixing of gender, since the omitted object to which the pronoun relates would not be kept in the mind of the average speaker and the idea of its gender would be entirely lost. The probable reason for the keeping of the feminine in such cases is that the expressions *pagarla*, etc., came to be a regular Italian locution and the speaker or writer adopted them as speech formulas without thinking of the gender of the omitted substantive.

bb.—Singular for the plural.

The masculine singular lo[2] is also used in referring to plural nouns in constructions where it stands in the predicate position, and expresses some attribute of a noun, just as is the case with an adjective.

cc.—*si* (= *ci*).

A very free use of the persons is the construction with *si*, the third person reflexive, for *ci*, the first person plural This construction is found only in W[3] and doubtless originated under the influence of the Lombard dialect[4].

A further mixing of persons may be seen in the use of the adverb *vi*[5], corresponding to the pronoun *vi*, for the third person dative singular and plural in constructions where it refers directly to objects or persons before mentioned[6]. This syntactical irregularity is probably a mere extension of the adverbial use of *vi* from the idea of place to that of persons and things. The adverb *vi* was already used in the sense of " there," " to that place," " to that part," etc., and by analogy to this third personal

---

[1] For example, in vederse*la* something like *la questione* is implied.

[2] *Cf.* ZZ, XIII, 276 : Che sono tutte malvagie, e se alcuna *lo* è meno, il suocero e la suocera *lo* saranno in sua vece.

[3] *Cf.* ur : Poi *si* traemo per la drita via ; Ciir, Noi *si* trovamo giunti su lextremo ; piiiir, Noi *se* partimo et prendemo el camino.

[4] *Cf.* Francesco Rinaldo, *Avvertimenti Grammaticali*. Modena, 1732 : " Alcuni, specialmente Lombardi, errano frequentemente *si*, che corrisponde al latino *se*, o *sibi*, per *ci*, che corrisponde *a nos*, o a *nobis* ; e così dicono *si partimmo*, *si feranmo*, in luogo di *ci partimmo*, *ci feranmo*."

[5] For the use of *ci* in similar constructions compare D'Ovidio, *Archiv. Glott. It.*, p. 78 ; Meyer-Lübke, *It. Gr.*, ¶ 371.

[6] *Cf.* M, p. 74 ; Fece a Marco una così fatta questione, credendo che Marco non *vi* potesse rispondere.

signification may have arisen its occasional substitution for the dative pronouns of the third person.

b.—Uses of *il*, *'l* and *lo* before the verb.

With reference to the position of *il* and *lo* in Dante and his contemporaries Groeber[1] says: "Es besteht vielmehr folgende Regel für den Gebrauch der zwei parallelen Artikel—und Pronominalformen in den ältesten Hdschn. der. Div. Com.: *lo, li* steht vor beliebigem Anlaut und hinter beliebigem Auslaut, *il, i* vor einfachem Consonanten und nur hinter vocalischem Auslaut." It will be noted that the rule quoted above, applies to *il* and *lo* both as articles and as pronouns. However, in consideration of the fact that *il* and *lo* as articles do not fall directly under a treatment of the same forms as pronouns, only the latter will be considered in this monograph.

To determine the law governing the position of *il*[2] and *lo* involves a discussion of the word preceding and the word following them in the sentence. Now, because it is an almost universal rule in Italian that the final letter of a word must be a vowel, the former question is practically restricted to the pronominal form permitted to stand after the particles *non, con, per, pur*, etc. For the texts examined, only one example of *il*[3] used after a final consonant has been noted, while the use of *lo* in this position is the regular Italian construction.

With reference to the word following *il* and *lo* the examples collected show that the use of *il*[4] before any given word was conditioned upon the fact that such a word should begin with a single consonant, whereas the adoption of *lo* before a word beginning with a single consonant was also permissible, and its use before a vowel or impure *s* was obligatory. Now, since the only position in

---

[1] *Zeit. fur. Rom. Phil.*, I, p. 108.

[2] Statements relative to the position of *il* and *lo* always include their corresponding plurals *i* and *gli* (*li*); however, *i* as the accusative plural only occurs five times in the texts examined (O 4, I).

[3] *Cf.* II, III, 151 : Non pur *il* porto, ecc.

[4] For the only examples found of *il* preceding a word beginning with impure *s* compare :

II, III, 195 : Iddio ringrazia, giugnendo le braccia,
   Che di tanto dolor si tosto il spoglia ;
II, I, 26, Vedendo che costui si poco *il* stima ;
LL, I, 93, Lo chiama al campo, ed alla pugna *'l* sfida.

which *il* could stand was when the word preceding it ended in a vowel, and the word following it began with a single consonant; and, because even in this position, *il*[1] and *lo* were used interchangeably, the parallel uses of these two forms in the construction just mentioned have been counted with results as shown by the table[2]. Such a résumé indicates that *il* was preferred for the most part in poetry and *lo* in prose, the former disappearing entirely from prose literature in the course of the sixteenth century and from poetry in the seventeenth century. Hence, we may conclude with the statement that Gröber's rule[3] relative to the position of *il* and *lo* as pronouns was not only the usage of Dante and his contemporaries, but was the practice of Tuscan authors until the pronominal function of *il* was finally lost in order to differentiate between the article and pronoun by the adoption of *il*[4] as an article and *lo* as a pronoun.

After personal forms of *essere* the conjunctive pronouns *il*[5] and *lo*[6] are used without variation for gender[7] or number[8] in the predicate sense of *it*, or *so*, for the purpose of representing the condition or quality of an adjective or noun already expressed[9].

c.—Position of atonic pronouns with finite verbs.

Mussafia[10] first announced the general principle, that in Old Italian atonic pronouns were always enclitic when depending on a finite verb standing at the beginning of the principal proposition, whether the sentence was declar-

---

[1] *Cf.* M, p. 23: Quelli *lo* mordea, e così *il* consumò.
[2] *Cf.* p. 40-41.
[3] *Cf.* p. 48.
[4] *Cf. il* giorno ; io *lo* vidi.
[5] *Cf.* WW, p. 259: Arminsi pure i Greci
    Furo ingrati ad Achille, e *il* sieno a Pirro ;
    YY, X, 243, *il* sarete.
[6] *Cf.* XX, I, 58, ...sarò padre
    Per compiacerti, come ora *lo* sono
    Per consigliarti.
[7] *Cf.* p. 34.
[8] *Cf.* p. 34.
[9] For the same construction in French compare Whitney's *French Grammar*. New York, 1886, pt. II, p. 246.
[10] *Cf. Miscellanea di Filologia e Linguistica.* Firenze, 1886, pp. 255-261.

ative[1], interrogative[2], imperative[3], subjunctive[4] used imperatively, an indicative[5] preceded by a vocative, or several[6] principal propositions succeeding one another without connectives[7].

On the other hand, if the principal proposition did not begin with a verb, it was the rule to place the atonic particles in proclitic position[8].

The reason for the use of enclitics with verbs standing at the beginning of the principal proposition is, according to Mussafia[9], because the early writers did not wish to begin the principal sentence with an unaccented particle.

In the fourteenth century[10] the unaccented pronouns began to disappear from enclitic position with finite verbs and with the exception of the second person singular and plural imperative and the first person plural imperative they ceased entirely to be employed in this construction about the middle of the seventeenth century.

d.—Position of atonic pronouns with infinitives.
aa.—Infinitives not dependent upon verbs.

When an infinitive is the subject[11] of a proposition, or depends upon a noun[12] or adjective[13], the unaccented particles are invariably written as enclitics.

---

[1] *Cf.* vidi*lo* for *lo* vidi.
[2] *Cf.* hot*ti* io mai ingiuriato?
[3] *Cf.* dim*mi*, dite*mi*, diciamo*gli*.
[4] *Cf.* piacia*ti*, rimangansene.
[5] *Cf.* amico mio, prego*ti*, ecc.
[6] *Cf.* andai da tuo fratello, diedi*gli* la lettera, pregai*lo*, ecc.
[7] As an explanation of expressions like *mi disse, mi rispose* Mussafia (*Miscellanea*, p. 258) says: "In questo caso l'orazione diretta rappresenta l'oggetto del *verbum dicendi*; e poiche il periodo comincia da questo oggetto, cessa l'obbligo dell'enclisi."
[8] *Cf.* io *lo* vidi; non *lo* vidi; non *ti* turbare; or *mi* di, donna, ecc.; non *lo* vedendo (or non vedendo*lo*). Here also belong constructions where the principal proposition was connected with another preceding, the first word of the proposition co-ordinated being any conjunction except *e* and *ma*; for example, one said io l'amo; perciò *lo* punisco, but riguardommi, ma sforzimi, etc. In like manner, when the pronoun relative adverb, or conjunction introducing a dependent clause was expressed, the verb being no longer at the head of the proposition, took the pronoun before it; as, l'uomo che *t*'ama, ecc.
[9] *Cf. Miscellanea*, p. 257.
[10] *Cf. Miscellanea*, p. 257.
[11] *Cf.* U, 1, 1; Il mandar*lo* fuori di casa nostra così infermo ne sarebbe gran biasimo.
[12] *Cf.* S, p. 330: Turno ha intendimento di cacciar*mi*.
[13] *Cf.* U, 5, 8: Io sono presto di far*lo*.

bb.—Infinitives depending on verbs.

When an infinitive depends upon an impersonal verb and only one atonic pronoun is expressed, this pronoun always stands before the principal verb[1], representing the *one* for whom the impersonal idea exists. On the contrary, if a second pronoun[2] is introduced, it is written in conjunction with the infinitive.

In all constructions where an infinitive is dependent upon a verb of *making*[3], *causing, seeing*[4], *hearing, permitting, letting* the conjunctive pronoun is placed before the independent verb, while it is always attached to the infinitive itself when the infinitive is governed by any transitive verb[5], except those just mentioned.

When an infinitive depends directly upon an intransitive verb, the atonic pronoun may be placed either before the main verb[6] or united with the infinitive[7], the two constructions being employed side by side (without apparent distinction) from the earliest texts to the present time.

If the preposition *di*[8] or *per* stands between the dependent infinitive and the governing verb, the *atonic pronoun is always attached to the infinitive.*

On the other hand, if the preposition *a*[9] precedes the infinitive, the conjunctive pronoun may go either with the principal verb or with the infinitive.

e.—Reflexives.

When the same person is both subject and object of a verb, the pronoun on which falls the action of the verb has a reflexive sense. For this purpose are used *mi, ti,*

---

[1] *Cf.* B, p. 139 : Ma *ti* conven partire ;
U, 1, 2, *mi* parea havere impiegata, &c.
[2] *Cf.* U, 2, 7 : *Mi* piace di raccontarvi.
[3] *Cf. Inf.* II, 70 : Io son Beatrice che *ti* faccio andare.
[4] *Cf. Inf.* I, 92 : A te convien tenere altro viaggio
Rispose, poi che lagrimar *mi* vide.
[5] *Cf.* U, 9, 5 : Credesse bene accender*lo*;
Y, p. 94 : pensa voler*lo* onorare ;
P, I, 234 : spero veder*lo* oggi ;
[6] *Cf.* U, 2, 3 : Io *ti* posso menare.
[7] *Cf.* LL, I, 98 : O che non puoi saper*lo*, o non schivarli.
[8] *Cf.* S, p. 291 : Desideriava *di* dar*la*.
[9] *Cf.* Y, p. 58 : La donna *lo* incominciò *a* pregare ;
KK, 11 : 380 *lo* venne *a* vedere ;
V, I, 76 : volle andare *a* veder*lo* ;
Y, p. 139 : e' cominciò *a* pregar*la*.

ci, vi, si[1], the plurals also being employed as reciprocals, meaning "each other," "one another," etc.

f.—Dative constructions.

aa.—Dative with verbs.

In Italian just as in Latin, the case of an indirect object denotes the person *to* or *for* which something exists or is done, designating the one affected or interested, and generally implying advantage or disadvantage.

Some of the principal verbs governing the dative case in Italian are:

1. Verbs of remembering[2], threatening[3], persuading, dissuading[4], conquering[5], pardoning[6].

2. All impersonal verbs[7].

3. In Italian as in Latin verbs accompanied by *satis*[8], *bene*[9], *male*[10] take the dative; *bene* and *male* being written apart from the verb in Italian, while in Latin the three forms were united with the verb (*cf. satisfacere, benefacere, malefacere*).

4. Verbs used with the prepositions *davante*[11], *avanti, innanzi, dietro, appresso*[12], *dirempetto, incontro*[13], *attorno, sotto*[14], *sopra, dinanzi*, etc., the preposition and verb being written separately in Italian but corresponding to the Latin dative after verbs compounded with *ante, post, prae, sub, super*, etc.

---

[1] The reflexive *si* must not be confounded with the particle *si* used as the sign of the passive signification of the verb or *si* meaning "one," "people," "they," etc. ; as, *si* racconta ; *si* scrive.

[2] *Cf.* P, I, 44 : Di chiamarmi a se non *le* ricorda ;
LL, II, 47, Di Bradamante più non *gli* sovviene.

[3] *Cf.* LL, III, 123 : E' *gli* minaccia, ecc.

[4] *Cf.* LL, V, 96 ; Molto *gli* dissuase Malagigi.

[5] *Cf.* LL, V, 260 : A Costantin del quale era sorella Costei si gittò a'piedi, *e gli* conquise.

[6] *Cf.* LL, IV, 4 :...... non *gli* perdono.

[7] *Cf.* parere, sembrare, bastare, dolere, valere, piacere, dispiacere, nocere, premere, convenire, degnare, mancare, cadere, calere, costare, gravare, giovare.

[8] *Cf.* LL, IV, 274 : Di questo Ferraù *le* satisfece.

[9] *Cf.* V, I, 13 : Che tu *le* voglia *bene*.

[10] *Cf.* V, I, 142 : *Mi* vuol *male*.

[11] *Cf.* LL, II, 125 : Ma la maga gentil *le* va *davante*.

[12] *Cf.* LL, II, 78 : Ruggier, *gli* e appresso....

[13] *Cf.* V, II, 208 : *Gli* venne *incontra*.

[14] *Cf.* NN, I, 12 : Il destrier *sotto gli* cade.

5. Transitive verbs governing the accusative and dative[1] case, when, together with the object of the action there is expressed the person or thing *to* or *for* which it is done.

bb.—Indirect object after adjectives.

Following the Latin construction, the Italian designates the object to which the quality of an adjective is directed by the use of the dative[2].

cc.—Dative of the possessor.

The verb *essere* is construed with a pronoun in the case of indirect object denoting the possessor. This usage is a pure Latinism and is limited to the authors indicated by DD[3], TT[4], WW[5], AAA[6].

dd.—Possessive strengthened by the dative

In Italian this construction is represented in three ways :

1. Both the dative and possessive pronoun are expressed[7];
2. When parts of the body are referred to, the masculine or feminine definite article[8] is substituted for the possessive ;
3. In certain idiomatic phrases where the sense is sufficiently clear the possessive pronoun and article are both omitted[9].

This strengthening of the possessive idea by the addition of the dative personal pronoun arose first in (Popular) Latin, according to the statement of the Latin grammarian

---

[1] *Cf.* V, I, 204 : *Le* domandò chi ella era ;
V, I, 130, *glie lo* mostro.

[2] *Cf.* A, p. 93r : Ed io più *le* starò sempre obbiente.

[3] *Cf.* p. 134 : Piu *gli* era io servidore.

[4] *Cf.* p. 104 : Io *gli* son pur amico.

[5] *Cf.* p. 260 : *Gli* sarò padre.

[6] *Cf.* 1, 146 : Padre *ti* sono.

[7] *Cf.* M, p. 40 : Poi *li* tolse il *suo* barlione ;
AA, p. 28, Se natura mi presta uom felice,
Subito morte *gli* usa il suo uffizzio.

[8] *Cf.* C, p. 49v : E *gli* ha spogliato il doloroso core ;
H, p. 195, lo Cardinale *si* levò lo capello ;
Z, nov. 4, raderòmmi la barba.

[9] *Cf.* I, p. 23 : Una lettera *gli* fue posta in mano ;
K, p. 3, si vide una colomba che *li* usciò di bocca.

Schmalz[1], who says: "Die Verstärkung des Poss. durch den Dat. des Pron. pers., Z. B. *meus mihi, tuus tibi*; Plaut. Cap. 50 *suo sibi servit patri*. Wir finden dies bei Plaut. Ter., kaum wohl bei Cicero (vgl. Seyffert Müller z. Lael. 11), höchstens Phil. 2, 96 *priusquam tu suum sibi venderes*, in Prosa demnach zuerst bei Vitruv 207, 18 R. dann bei Petron. 66 und Colum. 12, 41, 3, dann erst wieder bei den Archaisten und im Sp. L. bis in die späteste Zeit herab, vgl. Rönsch, Semas. Beitr. II, p. 52."

ee.—Dative of the agent.

Passive verbs take a dative of the agent[2] when it is desired to designate the person by whom the action is affected, to whom it relates or is of interest.

g.—Atonic pronouns of address.

The most common form of address in Old Italian was that by the use of the Latin *tu*. This form was employed from the beginning in prayer, personification, familiar discourse, address to children, servants, and lower animals, and was later used by Dante and others as a special term of dearness, displeasure and anger.

In the earliest Italian texts *tu* is already supplemented by *voi* used for the most part in addressing popes, kings, emperors, and other personages of distinction. The origin of the adoption of this plural form in addressing one individual belongs to Latin[3], appearing for the first time in the works of Jornandes[4], the historian of the Goths, who wrote about the middle of the sixth century.

Toward the end of the ninth century the plural was frequently used when speaking to kings and emperors, as

---

[1] *Cf.* Müller's *Handbuch der Klassichen Altertums-Wissenschaft*, München, 1890, vol. II., p. 573.

[2] *Cf.* F, p. 6 : Dei dire chosa che *ti* sia creduta ;
P, 1, 226 ; Di quest'altr'io : ed o pur non molesto
Gli sia 'l mio ingegno, e 'l mio lodar non spezze.

[3] *Cf.* Grimm, *Deutsche Grammatik*. Göttingen, 1837, vol. IV., p. 300.

[4] *Cf.* "*De Origine Actibusque Getarum.*" (In) *Monumenta Germaniae Historica*, Berolini, 1882, vol. V. Chap. 57 : Secumque deliberans ad principem ait : quamvis nihil deest nobis imperio *vestro* famulantibus, tamen, si dignum ducit pietas *vestra*, desiderium cordis libenter exaudiat. *Ibid.*, dirige me cum gente mea, si praecepis, ut et hic expensarum pondere careas et ibi, si adiutus a domino vicero, fama *vestrae* pietatis inradiet .... expedit namque, ut ego, qui sum servus *vester* et filius, si vicero, *vobis* domantibus regnum illud possedeam.

is seen in "Gesta Karoli[1]," where King Charles is usually entitled *vos*.

The explanation of the use of the plural *vos* for the singular *tu* is a difficult one. However, a suggestion that might account for it, is that it may have arisen by analogy to the use of *vos*, referring to collective[2] nouns or in addressing one individual of a class[3]. The carrying of the plural pronoun from constructions where it refers to a singular noun, expressing a collective or clan idea, to a singular noun applied to only one person is not an unnatural growth in popular speech. While the educated would use the plural form in the cases just indicated with the different individuals composing the class or collection of persons in mind, the peasant, knowing nothing of grammar, would naturally think of a collective noun as a single thing.

Then, because *vos* was already adopted in referring to certain nouns in the singular, but denoting a collection of persons the average speaker could see no reason why the same form should not stand for other singular nouns as well.

Perhaps a still more plausible analogy is that furnished by the first person plural. In the development of this construction, as in that of the second person plural, the first use of *nos* referring to one individual was doubtless in a collective sense. Just as *vos* was first employed in speaking to one man representing a body of persons, so was *nos* first used by Latin kings, emperors and princes in their official documents referring to the writer as the agent or representative of the people. Now, for the reason that the use of *nos*[4] for *ego* was already common among kings and emperors, when addressing the people, by analogy to this construction the subjects may have been led to adopt the plural *vos* in replying to their rulers.

---

[1] *Cf. Monumenta Germaniae Historica.* Hannoverae, 1829, vol. II., p. 733 : Dixerunt : Domine, ut nos in *vestro* nomine supra mediocritatem nostram honoraret ; p. 749, omnes dixerunt ad regem : Domine, ita estis inhonorati, sicut numquam anteriores *vestri*.

[2] *Cf.* Virgil, *Ae.* IX, 525 : *Vos*, o Calliope, precor adspirate canenti ; Liv. 7, 40, *Vos*, Romanus exercitus ; Hor, A. P., 292, *Vos*, o Pompilius Sanguis, carmen reprehendite.

[3] *Cf.* Silvius Italicus 16, 211 : Et *vos*, qui Tyriae registis Carthaginis arces, Hasdrubal, huc aures, huc quaeso advertite sensus ;
Cic. pro. Diot. 10, *Vos vestra* secunda fortuna, Castor, non potestis sine propinquorum calamitate esse contenti ?

[4] *Cf.* Grimm, *Deutsche Grammatik.* Göttingen, 1837, vol. IV., p. 299.

That the line of distinction between *tu* and *voi* had not, however, been clearly drawn, even at the beginning of the Italian period, is evidenced by the occasional confusion of the two forms in addressing the same person[1].

With reference to the use of abstract substantives as a form of address, Schmalz[2] says : " Schon Liv. lässt ihn in kühneren Wendungen zu, mehr noch Vell. Val. Max. Tac. u. Plin. min., und so entwickelt sich hieraus die offizielle Titulatur, Z. B. *Vestra serenitas*, etc. Vgl. Schöner, in act. sem. Erlang. II., p. 490 ff. Hierin leistete das konstantinische Zeitalter das Mögliche; ja die christl. Kirche eroberte sich nunmehr eine Titulatur, und *sanctitas tua* ist seit Ende IV. saec. stehende Anrede der Bischöfe.' Growing directly out of constructions where the abstract nouns above indicated were employed in address, is the substitution of *ella*, etc., for *voi*, etc. Instead of repeating the substantives *Santità, Eccellenza, Signoria*, etc., the speaker or writer used the third person feminine, *ella*[3] (corresponding to the gender of the omitted noun), for the same reason that one employs a pronoun instead of a noun in any other case.

On the date of the introduction of *ella* as the polite form of address in Italian, Blanc[4] remarks : " Erst mit dem 16. Jahrhundert fängt eine dritte, jetzt allgemein übliche Anrede durch *ella* an." Proving the incorrectness of this statement and showing that *ella* was used in such constructions at least two centuries before the time given by the grammarian just quoted is the occurrence of *le* (dat. of *ella*) in V[5], a novelist of the fourteenth century.

Ella was first employed only in addressing popes, to which signification it was restricted until toward the end of the sixteenth century, when its use was widened to include not only popes, but kings, emperors, princes and

---

[1] *Cf.* K, p. 76 : Con Dio v'accordarete, e vollio che *tue te* n'accordi con missere Jesù Cristo ; p. 82, amico mio, vollio che sappi che *tu* diei essere molto lieto, quando lo nostro Signore *vi* manda del vostro peccato alleggerimento.

[2] *Cf.* Müller's *Handbuch* München, 1890, vol. II., p. 535 d.

[3] *Cf.* KK, I, 156 : Ora io sono qui a' piedi di *Vostra Santità*, la quale e vero confessare, ch'*ella* faccia tanto di grazia di darmi licenza, acciocchè mi possa confessare.

[4] *Cf. It. Gr.*, p. 273.

[5] Vol. I., p. 211 : Et ella presentandosi davanti al Papa, gli disse Beatissimo Padre, *Vostra Santità* sa che io mai non *le* ho voluto manifestare di chi sieno nati questi figliuoli, ne ch'io mi sia.

other persons of eminence, being adopted still later as the usual address to ladies and as a mark of respect in general. At the beginning of the nineteenth century *lei*, the popular form for *ella*, was introduced into the literary language, and is the address most frequently heard in the popular speech of Tuscany to-day.

D.—*Discussion of double atonics.*

1.—Arrangement.

When a pronoun of the first or second person stands next to the third personal forms *lo*, etc., and *la*, etc., the general rule obtains for the whole of the texts examined that the indirect object precedes the direct[1]. However, in Old Italian, before the laws of position were definitely established, the direct object was often placed before the indirect[2].

Now, if the construction *me lo dice* is the regular Italian arrangement, how is the exception *lo mi dice* to be explained? Since in Latin, just as in Italian, the general law governing the position of the combinations under discussion was, that the indirect[3] should precede the direct object, while the opposite construction, with the direct[4] object coming first, was also permissible and not an infrequent usage with certain Latin authors, the most reasonable suggestion seems to be, that both constructions are a mere continuation of the Latin word-order. The final disappearance of constructions like *il vi dirò*, and the universal adoption of *ve lo dirò*, etc., instead may be attributed, first, to the numerical superiority of the latter word-arrangement over the former in Latin; and, secondly, to the general tendency in Italian to place the demonstrative forms after *mi* and *ti*, the conversion of *lo ti*, etc., > *te lo*, etc., arising not because the Italian preferred the dative before the accusative, but from a desire to place the pronouns of the first and second persons before those of the third person.

With reference to the arrangement of double forms,

---

[1] *Cf.* U, 2, 5 : Io *te 'l* vo dire.
[2] *Cf.* U, 1, 1 : Io *il vi* dirò.
[3] *Cf.* Terence, Eunuchus, 1053 : *Mihi illam* laudas? 897, *Tibi illam* reddat......?
[4] *Cf.* Terence, Eunuchus, 749 : *Hanc tibi* do donò; Andrea, 675 Ego, Pamphile, *hoc tibi* pro servitio debeo.

neither of which is *lo*, etc., or *la*, etc., the following statements may be made:
1. That *mi* and *ci* precede *ti* and *vi* ;
2. That *mi*, *ci*, *ti*, *vi* precede the reflexive *si*[1] ;
3. That the partitive *ne* follows all the other forms given (Nos. 1 and 2).

Conclusions.

As a résumé of the discussion upon the uses of atonic forms in atonic position the following conclusions may be drawn:

1. That of the nominatives *i'*, *i*, *no'*, *vo'*, *e'*, *gli*, *la*, *l'*, *le*, found in proclitic position in the texts consulted, *i'*, *i* and *e'* are Tuscan, while the other forms mentioned are dialectical or popular.

2. That the general law governing the elision of atonic vowels in hiatus in both Old and Modern Italian is, that *mi*, *ti*, *si*, *vi*, *lo*, *la* lose their vowel before any word beginning with a *vowel* or *h*, as contrasted with *gli* and the feminine plural *le*, which are elided only before similar vowels (*gli* before *i* and *le* before *e*), and the first person plural *ci*, which elides its *i* before *e* or *i* but keeps it before *a*, *o* and *u*. Up to the sixteenth century the proportion of exceptions to the rules above given, was less than 3%, while the increase of non-elided forms since that period has been so marked that with the present writers of Italy the use of a long or shortened form seems to be optional.

3. That *me*, *te*, *se* > *mi*, *ti*, *si* in enclitic position according to the general law that postonic $\bar{e} > i$[2], and that all enclitic pronouns were written in conjunction with the verb upon which they cast their accent, as a result of the general tendency manifest in orthography to represent faithfully the sounds of oral speech.

4. That, in Old Italian, *gli* was sometimes confused with the indirect feminine singular *le* on account of a tendency to preserve both Classic Latin ILLI (= masc. and fem. dat. sing.) and Popular Latin ILLAE (= fem. dat. sing.).

5. That, after personal forms of *essere*, *il* and *lo* are used for both genders and numbers in the sense of "it" or "so" when referring to some attribute or quality of a noun or adjective preceding.

---

[1] *Si* precedes the demonstrative forms *lo* and *la* (*cf. selo*, etc.).
[2] *Cf.* Meyer-Lübke, *It. Gr.*, ¶ 106.

6. That, idiomatic expressions like *vederla, pagarla, prenderla* are to be explained as speech formulas in which the feminine pronoun first arose when the feminine substantive to which it referred was either expressed or kept in mind, and that later, when the noun was entirely lost, the feminine pronoun was still preserved, because the expression had become a regular Italian locution, and was employed without thought of the gender.

7. That the dialectical use of *ci* and *vi* for the indirect singular and plural of third personal forms arose by analogy to the idea of a third person contained in the adverbs *ci* and *vi*, meaning " to it," " to them," etc., but not referring to anything before mentioned. Also that the further mixing of persons as seen in the occurrences of *si* for *ci* in W (*cf.* p. 47) is a borrowing from the Lombard dialect.

8. That Gröber's rule for the position of *il* and *lo* before the verb in Dante and his contemporaries ; namely, that *il* and *i* could follow any word ending in a vowel and precede any word beginning with a single consonant, while *lo* and *gli* (*li*) could follow any final letter and precede any initial letter, was the usage of Tuscan writers until the final disappearance of *il* (*cf.* p. 49).

9. That until the fourteenth[1] century atonic pronouns were attached to all forms of finite verbs standing at the beginning of the principal proposition, as a result of the fact that the early writers did not wish to begin the principal sentence with an unaccented particle[2].

10. That, when an atonic pronoun is governed by an infinitive, the former is joined as an enclitic to the latter, if the infinitive is the subject of a sentence, dependent upon a noun or adjective, or, if it depends upon a verb with the preposition *di* or *per* standing between the independent verb and the infinitive. However, if the infinitive depends upon a verb of *making, causing, seeing, hearing, feeling, letting, permitting*, the unaccented particles always stand in proclitic position, while they are attached to the infinitive when the latter follows immediately after and leans upon any other transitive verb except those just mentioned. Also, if the preposition *a* intervenes between the

---

[1] The first and second person imperative including the imperative use of *ecco* have retained the atonic pronouns in enclitic position because the force of command requires that the most important word shall stand first.

[2] Atonics were also occasionally attached to *dietro, addosso, dreto, che*.

principal verb and the dependent infinitive, or if the infinitive depends upon any intransitive verb, the placing of the atonic form in proclitic or enclitic position is optional.

11. That the Latin dative of the possessor, the possessive strengthened by the dative, the dative of the agent and the dative of interest, with the general idea of advantage and disadvantage, have been preserved in Italian.

12. That Latin *tu* has persisted in Italian as a term of endearment, displeasure, anger, hatred and inferiority, being employed most commonly in speaking to children, lower animals, and in supplicating the Deity.

With Jornandes in the middle of the sixth century begins the use of *vos* in addressing one person, being first applied only to emperors and kings, but later used as a title of respect in general.

In the fourteenth century *ella* was first adopted in supplicating popes, when referring back to the abstract substantive *Santità*, and toward the end of the sixteenth century its use was also extended to princes, nobles and others of similar rank, gradually supplanting *voi*, which latter form has been restricted to the address to the reader in books, address toward equals with whom one is on very familiar terms, or toward servants.

From the beginning of the eighteenth century dates the substitution of the popular form *lei* for the regular feminine nominative *ella*, the latter remaining, however, as the polite form of address in written speech, while the former belongs to the language of conversation.

13. That, when a pronoun of the first or second person is placed next to the third personal forms *lo*, etc., *la*, etc., the general rule is that the indirect object stands first. However, in Old Italian this rule was often reversed and the direct was made to precede the indirect object. Both of these constructions are directly traceable to the Latin (*cf.* p. 57), which generally shows the indirect object first, in combinations as above indicated, but not infrequent is the opposite usage, where the direct precedes the indirect object.

14. That in all other combinations of two atonics the first person always precedes the second and the first and second persons stand before the reflexive *si*[1].

---

[1] *Si* precedes the forms *lo* and *la* while *ne* follows all the other pronouns mentioned.

BIBLIOGRAPHY[1].

1.—TEXTS EXAMINED.

The following texts constitute the bibliography of this dissertation; they include the works of representative Tuscan authors from the middle of the thirteenth to the end of the nineteenth century. Throughout this monograph reference to the authors will be given by the use of the capital letters A, B, C, etc., standing opposite their names.

A.—Guittone d'Arezzo: (In) Sonetti e Canzoni di Diversi Antichi Autori Toscani in Dieci Libri Raccolte. Firenze, 1527.

B.—Chiaro Davanzati : (In) *Collezione di Opere inedite o rare*. III, 1-177; 261-265; 387-389.

C.—Cino da Pistoja: In A, pp. 47-60, 133, 134, 136, 137.

D.—Riccomano Jacopi : Libro della Tavola di Ric. Jac., edited by Carlo Vesme (in) *Archivio Storico Italiano*, 3ª serie, vol. XVIII. (1873).

E.—Dante da Maiono: In A, pp. 72-88, 133, 137, 139, 140.

F.—Albertano di Brescia : Volgarizzamento dei Tratti Morali di Albertano Giudice di Brescia. Fatto innanzi al 1278. Trovato da S. Ciampi. Firenze, 1832.

G.—Ricordi di una Famiglia Senese del secolo decimoterzo (1231-1243). Pub. by G. Milanesi in *Archiv. Stor. Ital.*, Appendice, Vol. V. Firenze, 1847.

H.—Ranieri Sardo : Cronaca Pisana di Ran. Sar., Dall. Anno 962 sino al 1400. Pub. by F. Bonaini in *Archiv. Stor. Ital.*, Vol. VI., parte 2ª, pp. 73-244. Firenze, 1845.

I.—Fiore di filosofi e di molti savi, attribuito a Brunetto Latini. Testo in parte inedito, citato dalla Crusca, e ridotto a miglior lezione da Antonio Cappelli : (In) *Scelta di curiosità letterarie o rare*, Vol. LXIII. Bologna, 1865.

---

[1] As the most of the grammatical and syntactical changes in the Italian language took place before the sixteenth century, fewer texts have been examined for the Modern than for the Old Italian.

J.—Lettere Volgari del secolo XIII, scritte da Senesi. Pub. by Paoli e Piccolomini in *Scelta, ecc.*, CXVI. Bologna, 1871.

K—Dodici Conti morali d'Anonimo Senese. Testo inedito del secolo XIII, pubb. da Zambrini. *Scelta, ecc.*, IX. Bologna, 1862.

L.—Conti di Antichi Cavalieri: (In) *Giornale Storico della Letteratura Italiana*, Vol. III., pp. 192-217. Torino, 1884.

M.—Le cento Novelle Antiche. Milano, 1825.

N.—Guido Cavalcanti: Le Rime di Guid. Cav. Testo critico pubb. dal Prof. Nicola Arnone. Firenze, 1881. Also in A.

O.—Dante: La Divina Commedia di Dante Alighieri, edited by G. A. Scartazzini, Milano, 1896.

P.—Petrarca: Rime di Pet. 2 vols. Padova, 1819.

Q.—Jacopo di Pistoja: Statuti dell'Opera di S. Jacopo di Pistoja, volgarizzati l'anno MCCCXIII da Mazzeo di Ser Giovanni Bellebuoni, con due inventari del 1340 e del 1401. Pubb. da S. Ciampi. Pisa, 1814.

R.—Bindo Bonichi: Rime di Bind. Bon. da Siena. *Scelta, ecc.*, LXXXII. Bologna, 1867.

S.—Guido da Pisa: Fiore di Italia. Bologna, 1824.

T.—Ricordi di Miliadusso Baldiccione de' Casalberti. Pubb. da Bonaini e Polidori in *Archiv. Stor. Ital.*, Appendice, Vol. VIII., pp. 17-71. (First record 1339, last 1382.) Firenze, 1850.

U.—Boccaccio: Il decamerone. Impresso in Firenze per li heredi di Philippo di Giunta nell'anno del Signore, M. D. XXVII. A di XIIII del mese d'aprile.

V.—Giovanni Fiorentino: Il Pecorone. 2 vols. Milano, 1804.

W.—Fazio degli Uberti: Opera di Faccio Degliuberti Fiorentino Chiamato Ditta Mundi. Venetia, 1501.

X.—Forestani : Storia d'una Fanciulla Tradita da un suo Amante. Di Messer Simone Forestani da Siena. Ed. da Zambrini. *Scelta, ecc.*, VI. Bologna, 1862.

Y.—Sercambi : Novelle di Giovanni Sercambi. Ed. da Alessandro d'Ancona. *Scelta, ecc.*, CXIX. Bologna, 1871.

Z.—Sacchetti : Novelle. 3 vols. Milano, 1804.

AA.—Zenone da Pistoja : La Pietosa Fonte. Ed. da Zambrini. *Scelta, ecc.*, CXXXVII. Bologna, 1874.

BB.—I Cantari di Carduino ; giuntovi quello di Tristano e Lancielotto. Pubb. per cura di Pio Rajna. *Scelta, ecc.*, CXXXV. Bologna, 1873.

CC.—Leon Battista Alberto : Hecatomphila di Messer L. B. Alb. Vineggia, 1534.

DD.—Gambino d'Arezzo : Versi. Ed. da Gamurrini. *Scelta, ecc.*, CLXIV. Bologna, 1878.

EE.—Poliziano : Stanze, l'Orfeo ed altre Poesie. Milano, 1808.

FF.—Burchiello : (In) I Sonetti del Burchiello et di Messer Antonio Alamanni. Firenze, 1552.

GG.—Lorenzo de'Medici : Poesie. Firenze, 1859.

HH.—Hieronimo Benivieni : Tancredi, Principe di Salerno. Novella in rima di H. Beniv. Fiorentino. Ed. da Zambrini. *Scelta, ecc.*, XXVIII. Bologna, 1865.

II.—Bojardo : Orlando Innamorato (Berni's Rifacimento). 4 vols. Milano, 1806.

JJ.—Antonio Alamanni : Sonetti di Messer Ant. Alamanni Cittadino Fiorentino. In FF, pp. 72-83.

KK.—Benvenuto Cellini : Opere. Milano, 1806. Vols. I., II., Vita di Ben. Cel. da lui medesimo scritta.

LL.—Ariosto : Orlando Furioso. 5 vols. Milano, 1812.

MM.—Machiavelli : Opere. Milano, 1804. Vol. I., Il Principe.

NN.—Pietro Bembo : Opere. Milano, 1808. Vol. I., Gli Asolani.

OO.—Torquato Tasso : Aminta. Parigi, 1655.
PP.—Batecchio, Commedia di Maggio. Composto per il Pellegrino Ingegno del Fumoso della Congrega de' Rozzi. Scelta, ecc., CXXII. Bologna, 1871.
QQ.—Guarini : Il Pastor Fido. Venetia, 1602.
RR.—Giulio Ottonelli : Negoziazione alla Corte di Spagna. Scelta, ecc., XXVII. Bologna, 1863.
SS.—Guido Ubaldo Bonarelli : Filli di Sciro. Pub. by Baldini. Ferrara, 1607.
TT.—Michelagnolo Buonarotti (il giovane) : La Tancia, Commedia Rusticale. (In) *Teatro Italiano Antico*. Vol. X. Milano, 1812.
UU.—Alessandro Tassoni : La Secchia Rapita. 2 vols. Parigi, 1766.
VV.—Fantozzi Parma : Diario del Viaggio Fatto in Inghilterra nel 1639 dal Nunzio Pontificio Rossetti, scritto da Domenico Fantozzi. Parma. Pubb. dal Prof. Giuseppe Ferraro, (in) *Scelta, ecc.*, CCXII. Bologna, 1885.
WW.—Apostolo Zeno : Andromaca. (In) *Teatro Classico Italiano Antico e Moderno*, vol. III., pp. 255-269. Lipsia, 1829.
XX.—Scipione Maffei : Merope. Boston, 1890. Pub. by Librairie Hachette et Cie., London, Paris, Boston.
YY.—Carlo Goldoni : Collezione delle Commedie di Carlo Goldoni. Prato, 1827-29. Vol. I., pp. 1-75, Teatro Comico, vol. X., pp. 239-327, Il Torquato Tasso.
ZZ.—Pietro Metastasio : Opere. Firenze, 1819. Vol. I., pp. 1-84, Didone Abbandonata ; Vol. XIII.
AAA.—Vittorio Alfieri : (1) Opere scelte. Milano, 1818. Vol. I., pp. 118-176, Antigone.—(2) Opere di Vitt. Alfieri. Padova, 1809. Vol. VI., pp. 1-94, Saul.
BBB.—Alessandro Manzoni : I promessi Sposi, Storia Milanese del Secolo XVII. (In) *Collezione de' migliori Autori Italiani Antichi e Moderni,* Vol. I. Pub. by Baudry. Parigi, 1844.

CCC.—Leopardi: Paralipomeni della Batracomiomachia. Parigi, 1842.

DDD.— Edmondo De Amicis : La Vita Militare. Firenze, 1869.

EEE.—Matilde Serao : Dal Vero. Milano, 1890.

FFF.—Giosuè Carducci : (1) Odi Barbare. Bologna, 1888.
—(2) Studi Letterari. Bologna, 1893.

2.—GENERAL.

1.—Meyer-Lübke : *Italienische Grammatik.* Leipzig, 1890.

2.—Meyer-Lübke : *Grammaire des Langues Romanes.* Paris, 1890.

3.—*Archivio Glottologico Italiano.* G. I. Ascoli.

4.—*Zeitschrift für Romanische Philologie.* Gustav Gröber, Halle.

5.— C. N. Caix: *Origini della Lingua Poetica Italiana.* Firenze, 1880.

6.—Blanc : *Grammatik der Italiänischen Sprache.* Halle, 1844.

7.—Monaci : *Crestomazia Italiana dei Primi Secoli.* Città di Castello, 1889.

8.—Louis Emil Menger: *Historical Development of the Possessive Pronouns in Italian.* Baltimore, 1893.

9.—Francesco Fortunio : *Regole Grammaticali, della Volgar Lingua.* Siena, 1533.

10.—Jacopo Gabriello : *Regole Grammaticali.* Venetia, 1548.

11.—Biagoli : *Grammaire Italienne.* Paris, 1819.

12.—Veneroni : *Le Maître Italien.* Paris, 1796.

13.—Mugnozzi : *Les Elémens de la Langue Italienne.* Paris, 1783.

14.—Fornaciari : *Grammatica Italiana.* Firenze, 1891.

15.—Jacomo Cabriele: *Regole Grammaticali.* Venetia, 1545.
16.—Caix: *Osservazioni sul Vocalismo Italiano.* Firenze, 1875.
17.—Francesco Rinaldo: *Avvertimenti Grammaticali.* Modena, 1732.
18.—A. Mussafia: (In) *Miscellanea di Filologia e Linguistica.* Firenze, 1886.
19.—Grimm: *Deutsche Grammatik.* Göttingen, 1837.
20.—Etienne: *Grammaire de l'Ancien Français.* Paris, 1895.
21.—Müller: *Handbuch der Klassischen Altertums-Wissenschaft*, 1890.
22.—Jornandes: *Romana et Getica*, (In) *Monumenta Germaniae Historica*, vol. V. Berolini, 1882.
23.—Schwan: *Grammatik des Altfranzösischen.* Leipzig, 1893.
24.—Karl Bartsch: *Chrestomathie Provençale.* Elberfeld, 1868.

LIFE.

I, Oliver Martin Johnston, was born near Bastrop, Louisiana, October 17, 1866. I was graduated from Mississippi College with the degree of A.B. in June, 1890; the following year I was Principal of the Preparatory Department in the college above mentioned; the two succeeding years I held the professorship of English and History in the same college. Resigning the latter position in June, 1893, I entered the Johns Hopkins University in October of the same year, choosing Italian and French as my principal and first subordinate subjects, in which I followed the courses given by Professor A. Marshall Elliott, Doctor Louis Emil Menger, and Professor A. Rambeau. As a second subordinate subject I studied History under Professor H. B. Adams, my examination in this subject being on the Renaissance in Italy. The summer of 1894 I spent in Paris, engaged in Modern French studies and in the preparation of my thesis. From May to August of 1895 I continued in Paris my Modern French studies and the collection of material for my thesis; from August to October of this year I spent in Florence, Italy, doing special work in Modern Italian. During the last two years of my course I have followed the lectures of Professor Elliott and Doctor Menger, and I take this opportunity to express to both of them my appreciation of the able instruction, timely suggestions and wise guidance which they have so constantly given me in my work.

From January to June of 1895 I held a Scholarship in the Romance Department of the Johns Hopkins University, and since June, 1895, I have held a Fellowship in this university.

BALTIMORE, MARYLAND,
  May 5, 1896.

www.ingramcontent.com/pod-product-compliance
Lightning Source LLC
Chambersburg PA
CBHW020227090426
42735CB00010B/1608